Spirituality and Personal Maturity

Joann Wolski Conn

Integration Books

paulist press/new york and mahwah

For Walt

Library of Congress Cataloging-in-Publication Data

Conn, Joann Wolski.
   Spirituality and personal maturity / Joann Wolski Conn.
      p.   cm. — (Integration books)
   Includes bibliographies.
   ISBN 0-8091-3074-2
   1. Emotional maturity—Religious aspects—Christianity.
   2. Spirituality.   3. Feminist theology.   I. Title.   II. Series.
   BV4509.5.C658   1989
   248—dc20   89-33661
                                                        CIP

Published by Paulist Press
997 Macarthur Boulevard
Mahwah, New Jersey 07430

Printed and bound in the
United States of America

Contents

Integration Books

STUDIES IN PASTORAL PSYCHOLOGY,
THEOLOGY, AND SPIRITUALITY
Robert J. Wicks, General Editor

also in this series
Clinical Handbook of Pastoral Counseling
edited by R. Wicks, R. Parsons, and D. Capps
Adolescents in Turmoil, Parents Under Stress
by Richard D. Parsons
Pastoral Marital Therapy
by Stephen Treat and Larry Hof
The Art of Clinical Supervision
edited by B. Estadt, J. Compton and M. Blanchette
The Art of Passingover
by Francis Dorff, O. Praem
Losses in Later Life
by R. Scott Sullender
Pastoral Care Emergencies
by David K. Switzer

Foreword

The Old and New Testaments are filled with the passion of persons, in covenant with God, trying to fulfill their destiny. They embody the meaning and adventure of the word *relationship;* their exploits are filled with the drama of facing themselves, interacting with their communities, and—in many forms— meeting their God.

Today, this challenging endeavor is still a calling for those who wish to seek both human and spiritual maturity by passionately seeking to understand and live out the truth with others. Yet, dominance by archaic superegos, outdated societal norms, and unhelpful spiritual imagery prevent growth toward God. In place of the vibrant characters of sacred scriptures, many of us are left wrapped in unnecessary psychological defenses and pulled down, rather than guided, by our theological traditions.

In reference to the great theologian Karl Rahner, John McDargh (1985) notes: "Every theology . . . is first an anthropology or, if you will, a 'theological anthropology' and hence whatever genuinely clarifies the human condition potentially contributes to the theological project." In Joann Wolski Conn's book *Spirituality and Personal Maturity* we are struck by a recognition of this fact and concrete measures are provided to encourage the process of self-discovery.

By focusing on psychological theory, reflecting on Christian spirituality, and providing detailed clinical illustrations, she guides us through a search for a better understanding of, and approach to, psycho-spiritual maturity. By acknowledging the interplay between grace and personal freedom and the roles of both relationship and autonomy, she promotes a deep desire to understand humans as a way of understanding God.

Spirituality and Personal Maturity is an unusual book with respect to its scope and design. Certainly, it is an ideal work for

1

persons in professional pastoral ministry—whether they be pastors, directors of religious education, youth ministers, or professional pastoral therapists/counselors. However, this book which is woven with both hopeful psychological insights and a rich Carmelite spirituality is really for all adults grappling with their own faith development; it is indirectly quite a prayerful work which calls us to find God by rejoicing in human nature and the offerings of God that are contained in an appreciation of the ordinary aspects of life. As a matter of fact, I learned not only from the statements made by Dr. Joann Wolski Conn in each chapter, but also by the attitude and spirit of personal/social justice and concern that I felt pervading the entire book. She has taught me that human understanding and metanoia should, and can, indeed go hand in hand.

Robert J. Wicks

Reference

McDargh, John. "Theological Uses of Psychology: Retrospective." *Horizons,* 12/2 (1985), 251.

Introduction

This book explores the conviction that Christian spirituality and human maturity are integrated in a way that is mutual and reciprocal. That is, they can be understood as identical in some ways, without reducing God's grace to humanistic psychology. In the practical terms that concern pastoral counselors and spiritual directors, this means that promoting human maturity *is* promoting Christian development, and supporting authentic Christian life *is* contributing to psychological health. This conviction can only be reasonably supported, however, on one condition. Christian spirituality and personal maturity are truly integrated, not merely connected by subordinating one to the other, if and only if they have the same goal or model of maturity. Presentation and evaluation of a model that can be common to spiritual and psychological maturity is the aim of this book.

Examples from the theological debate about the relationship of nature and grace illustrate the distinction between subordinating and truly integrating. God's grace, meaning God's offer of loving relationship and a sharing in God's own life, is freely given and initiates this relationship. On this point all theologians have agreed. As *The Westminster Dictionary of Christian Spirituality* (1983, pp. 179–180) explains, debate centers on our part in this relationship. Because humans cannot earn God's love and do not deserve it, we wonder about the place of our human freedom and the significance of our natural patterns of human thought and choice. For example, can we actively deepen or ensure this union with God? Through the years theologians have debated this complex question and from these discussions have come two basic trends. From Augustine, through Luther and Calvin has come a reformation emphasis on the primacy of God's action. Overwhelming conviction of human nature as basically sinful or incapacitated resulted in attributing the entire responsibility for conversion, the good life, and ultimate salvation to God's free grace, as J. Patout Burns (1985) explains. From the eastern fathers of the church and from Thomas Aquinas has come another emphasis, that of grace as the "divinization" of humanity and the consequent theme of "grace building on nature" or "grace working through nature" to complete human potential. Although the second trend appears to correspond to the integration of grace and nature, and the Augustinian trend to correspond to a subordination of nature to grace, in fact both trends have usually been explained in terms of subordination. Some practical examples will clarify the implications of this subordinationist approach.

Inspired by the Augustinian theology of God's primacy in the Christian life, Andrew and Pamela, who have had a difficult marriage for the past seven years, concluded that union with God should eliminate their psychological problems.

They spoke to their pastor a few times in general terms about their different interests, background, and conflicting ideals of a happy marriage. Kindness drew them closer to church activities and eventually to the instructions offered by the charismatic prayer group in their congregation. After several sessions they joined the group and experienced being "born again" in the Spirit. Now, they believe, their marriage problems will disappear because, as Pamela says, "surely we are one in the Spirit of God, so we will be one in our married life." The debatable issue here is not the authenticity of their experience, nor the power of God's spirit to create healing and forgiveness. Rather, the conclusion to be questioned is the interpretation of the religious and psychological dimensions of this experience in terms of subordination.

Although inspired by the theology of grace working through nature, Janice and Arthur, too, interpret their Christian experience in terms of subordination. They assume a need for the subordination of their "lower nature" to grace's "higher call to self-sacrifice." Janice, in her mid-thirties, is the single-parent of three children and is completing the college degree she interrupted when her first child was born. A fervent Episcopalian, she decided to minor in religious studies and enrolled in a course on the theology of prayer. Involvement in this topic began to make Janice uncomfortable about the amount of attention she devoted to her own study, rest, and friends at college. "Good heavens," she concluded, "I seem to be falling into the 'self-fulfillment thing.' How could I be so immature and selfish?" Janice now considers giving up the college degree that she wants and returning to the volunteer work that she dislikes. Janice assumes that the gospel call to self denial is an extrinsic "higher demand" for conduct that human nature itself finds repugnant. She images the "self" as a well of needs and desires to be satisfied or denied. Arthur, a Catholic priest in his forties, finished his yearly retreat by resolving "to make God, not myself, the center of my life." He is puzzled about what action to take in order to live out this resolution since he is already giving most of his time to the needs of his parishioners. He is suspicious about time given to the enjoyment of friends in the parish and wonders whether he is "just giving in to his need for affection and affirmation." His image of the self parallels Janice's: a complex of needs to be satisfied or denied. Arthur's image of God's relationship to humanity is that of a loving Father competing for Arthur's affection for creatures. His image is one that demands all; that is, for God to be central Arthur must deny his needs; ideally, he freely subordinates himself to God's grace in his life. Arthur's assumptions, like Janice's, need to be questioned and evaluated.

My criticism of subordination as an adequate framework for interpreting the relationship of Christian spirituality and human maturity stems from both theological and psychological concerns. Theology is my primary norm of evaluation. More precisely, a feminist theology of God's relationship to humanity is this book's norm for judging the adequacy of theological positions and its critique of domination and subordination are central to that position, as I have explained in detail in "A Discipleship of Equals: Past, Present and Future" (1987). A summary of the basic insights of this position will suffice here since additional explanations are presented later in the book as they are used in case studies from pastoral counseling and spiritual direction.

Feminist theology of grace and of God are an expression of the faith of the Christian community which is rooted both in women's experience of mutual relationships of sisterhood and in rejection of the male-centered theology of God which projects onto God the control and domination exerted by authoritarian rulers. As Judith Plaskow (1980, p. 172) explains, feminist theology understands grace neither as "shattering," as by an authoritarian father-judge (Niebuhr), nor as quietistic "acceptance," as by a stereotypically understanding mother (Tillich), neither as subordination nor participation which threatens the boundaries of the self. God, as feminist theologians Anne Carr (1988), Sally McFague (1987), Rosemary Ruether (1983), and Sandra Schneiders (1986) explain, is more appropriately understood and experienced as Friend whose person is never fully known, yet is comforting and at home with us; one who urges our freedom and autonomy in decision yet who is present in the community of interdependence and, in fact, creates it; one who is revealed in Jesus who rejects every form of domination, calling us not servant but friend.

My criticism of subordination is rooted also in psychological concerns about the consequences of that position. In the case of Andrew and Pamela, for example, serious difficulties will surely arise and opportunities for greater love will be missed. If they assume that grace cancels their weaknesses and problems, they will deny their differences of opinion and avoid dealing with conflict. This can only lead to deeper antagonism. They will miss opportunities to explore the long-term consequences of the new sense of forgiveness and mutual love which arises from authentic religious experience. In the case of Janice and Arthur, the absence of a developmental model of the self gives them no standard by which to discern appropriate denial. Are they to deny their preferences or opinions? If so, is this not compulsive fear of offending people or simple conformity to social or religious roles? Can one have self-sacrifice if one has little or no boundaries of self-identity? Subordination of human maturity to Christian spirituality leaves Christian life quite vulnerable to psychology's classical, legitimate criticism of religion: the persistent tendency to promote dependence, reinforce authoritarianism, and be suspicious of any pleasure.

These theological and psychological reasons lead me to reject the model of subordination and prefer, instead, to explore the theology of "grace working through nature" in terms of the possibility of integrating Christian spirituality and human maturity. The search for a model of integration means a desire to demonstrate my conviction that they are inseparable, parallel, even identical in basic ways. They are distinguished and evaluated according to norms that are theological. That is, Christian spirituality serves as the primary interpreter and evaluator of human maturity, although spirituality certainly seeks evaluation from psychology. They are identical in basic ways if it can be demonstrated that they have the same goal, the same criterion of maturity. This is not an easy task since the common assumption is that spirituality's goal is self-sacrifice and humanity's goal is the opposite: self-fulfillment. Therefore, this question of the possibility of a common goal will be the central focus of this book.

Seeing the parallels between spirituality and human maturity is helpful but it is not the same as finding a deeper integration in terms of a common goal. Yet examining the work of two experts who do see parallels will raise the questions that demand further searching. The story of Ruth Burrows and the research of Mary Wolff-Salin exemplify a recognition of parallels between human growth and religious development in one's own life (Burrows), and an attempt to spell out these parallels (Wolff-Salin).

In the story of her life as a contemplative Carmelite nun, Ruth Burrows (1981) explains how the insight into the parallels between spiritual and human development became so important to her. She tells of a lifetime of struggle with depression, self-doubt, and longing to be loved, until she eventually found a way to combine two things that she once considered incompatible: using her talent for leadership and surrendering entirely to God. Burrow's central message is encouragement to learn, as she did, to see God at work in all aspects of life. Learn to see God working, she says, not merely in exterior events but in your own hearts, in the difficulties of temperament, in all that you were taught to see as outside God's range or as an obstacle to God. It is here that we need to see God most of all, she maintains, because this is how we deepen our exposure to God. From her experience she learned that we reach God not by abandoning means of personal development such as intellectual formation, creative work and intimate friendship; rather, these are necessary. To cut ourselves off from the maturing process, to shirk personal growth under cover of the cliché "God alone," is, in fact, to escape from God because God is not glorified in half-persons. The more we open ourselves to life, she concludes, the more we are opening ourselves to surrender to God.

Burrows' story corrects false teachings which imply that growth in relationship to God comes at the price of repressing human growth, yet its generalities leave serious questions unanswered. Why did her spiritual life flourish when she attended to human growth? Is it because God desires that we have more self-fulfillment than we might think? Is it because she misunderstood the areas of appropriate self-denial? Precisely how can spiritual directors and pastoral counselors assist people to see what Burrows now sees? What model of self and of maturity can not only support Burrows' conclusions but also demonstrate concretely the integration which Burrows' personal story reveals? These are the questions I answer in this book.

Another approach to the issue of parallels between human growth and religious development is that of the psychologist Mary Wolff-Salin. In *No Other Light: Points of Convergence in Psychology and Spirituality* (1986) she demonstrates how some points of both Freud's and Jung's descriptions of psychological growth converge with descriptions of spiritual theologians. For instance, she notices the parallels between Jung's description of "facing and befriending our shadow" and Merton's explanation of spiritual self-knowledge. She also sees correlations between the way psychologists examine "projections" or deal with "transference" and the way spiritual directors exercise "discretion." She concludes that, although they may differ on the theoretical level regarding many topics such as God and the ultimate meaning of humanity, on the level of experience there are valid parallels or even points of convergence between psychology and spirituality.

Wolff-Salin demonstrates that differences on the theoretical level need not preclude one from seeing parallels on the experiential level. For me, the theoretical question persists, nevertheless, because inconsistent theory breeds inconsistent practice. Is there a theory of human maturity that is absolutely compatible with the theory of Christian maturity? If so, then we could go beyond simply noting parallels in experience that transcend theoretical contradictions. We could have theoretical consistency, also. If so, pastoral counselors and spiritual directors would have a concrete model that supports practical integration of spirituality and human maturity.

Method

Because I am convinced that spiritual maturity does not contradict or frustrate human maturity, even though past experience shows that spiritual theology often bred immaturity, I begin with this issue. Chapter 1 surveys the history of Christian spirituality examining how the tradition understood Christian maturity as *relationship*. It explains the shift in consciousness evident in Vatican Council II and stresses new, emerging issues. Chapter 2 continues attention to the issue of relationship but shifts the focus from spirituality to psychology. It explains Carol Gilligan's model of maturity as relationship and evaluates its usefulness for integrating human and spiritual development. Chapter 3 explains why the constructive-developmental model of Robert Kegan is more useful than Gilligan's model for integrating spiritual and human maturity. Chapter 4 uses case studies to demonstrate the value of Kegan's model of maturity for integration in pastoral counseling. Chapter 5 expands the focus of integration to include spiritual direction and uses cases, again, to show similarities and differences between pastoral counseling and spiritual direction. Chapter 6 continues attention to integration in both spiritual direction and pastoral counseling by focusing on a single issue: psychological depression (as interpreted by Robert Kegan) and spiritual darkness (as interpreted by John of the Cross), noting the similarities and differences in terms of movement toward maturity. The Conclusion notes implications and challenges for the ministries of pastoral counseling and spiritual direction.

This book would not have been possible without the support of many people. I want to thank my colleagues in Neumann College's graduate program in pastoral counseling, especially Rick Parsons for insights gained through team-teaching with him, Barbara Price for her interest and professional assistance, and my students for their enthusiasm for both learning and pastoral ministry. My thanks extend also to my colleagues in the humanities division who make my working environment so enjoyable. Bob Wicks, the series' editor, has given consistent support and valuable suggestions. Teresa Byrne was very generous in assisting with preparation of the manuscript. I am profoundly grateful to the women who nurture my faith by sharing their faith-life with me in spiritual direction.

For their careful reading and constructive comments on an earlier draft of this book I want to thank Elizabeth Dreyer, Constance FitzGerald, Margaret Gorman, Patricia Cooney Hathaway, Joan Koliss, Sandra Schneiders, and Mary Jo Weaver. Walt Conn, my husband, not only offered creative ideas and questions at every phase of writing, but also gives me the loving partnership which invigorates this and every other aspect of my life.

References

Burns, J. Patout. "Grace: The Augustinian Foundation." In *Christian Spirituality: Origins to the Twelfth Century,* edited by Bernard McGinn and John Meyendorff. New York: Crossroad, 1985.

Burrows, Ruth. *Before the Living God.* Denville, New Jersey: Dimension Books, 1981. Orig., 1975.

Carr, Anne. *Transforming Grace.* San Francisco: Harper & Row, 1988.

Conn, Joann Wolski. "A Discipleship of Equals: Past, Present, Future." *Horizons* 14/2 (Fall 1987), 231–261.

McFague, Sallie. *Models of God.* Philadelphia: Fortress, 1987.

Plaskow, Judith. *Sex, Sin and Grace.* Washington, D.C.: University Press of America, 1980.

Ructher, Rosemary. *Sexism and God-Talk.* Boston: Beacon, 1983.

Schneiders, Sandra. *Women and the Word.* New York: Paulist, 1986.

The Westminster Dictionary of Christian Spirituality. Philadelphia: Westminster, 1983, s.v. "Grace."

Wolff-Salin, Mary. *No Other Light: Points of Convergence in Psychology and Spirituality.* New York: Crossroad, 1986.

Chapter 1

Spirituality

The term spirituality refers to both a lived experience and an academic discipline. For Christians, it means one's entire life as understood, felt, imagined, and decided upon in relationship to God, in Christ Jesus, empowered by the Spirit. It also indicates the interdisciplinary study of this religious experience, including the attempt to promote its mature development.

The word spirituality, as Sandra Schneiders (1986) has explained, has an interesting history. Originally a term from Paul's letters referring to all Christians' life according to the Holy Spirit, it gradually came to mean that life as the special concern of "souls seeking perfection" rather than as the common experience of all Christians. Seeking perfection became a matter of the individual, interior practice of special spiritual exercises requiring careful guidance by experts. Emphasis was on affectivity and obedience to authority; critical reflection was suspect. The contemporary theological shift toward a recovery of sources in scripture, history, and liturgy has demonstrated how distorted the previous understanding had become. The last section of this chapter will elaborate on the current use of this term. The first two sections will review the history of the way Christian spiritual tradition interpreted maturity, the goal of Christian life.

I. History of Spirituality

A. Biblical Spirituality

Paul's Letters. Paul understands his life and that of every Christian as life "in Christ." Faith in God's action in raising Christ incorporates us into Christ who pours out his Spirit,

13

enabling us to recognize God as "Abba." Thus, Paul's religious experience is one of seeing the risen Lord, feeling empowered by the Spirit to witness to God's re-creation of all women and men in Christ: Jew and Greek, slave and free.

For Paul, the experience of day to day life in Christ centers on bearing one another's burdens, which is fulfilling the whole law; giving and receiving the Spirit's gifts which build up the body of Christ; offering ourselves as living sacrifices of praise and thanksgiving for God's overwhelming love for us in Christ—the love that nothing can ever separate us from. Eating the meal of unity and love, remembering Christ Jesus, renews our faith in God's re-creating action in Christ, the new Adam, and in us.

In the beginning of Paul's life in Christ his experience of the risen Christ led him to concentrate on proclaiming the power of the resurrection. Later, his experience of struggle and failure in his ministry led him to appreciate more deeply the mystery of Christ's passion. Thus, his mature experience was one of ever deeper participation in the entire paschal mystery, of loving trust even unto death so that the power of God manifest in Jesus' weakness might be manifest also in Paul's weakness and in ours.

Mark's Gospel. Concerns and questions of the community influence the focus of this and every gospel. The faith-experience of Mark's community centers on Jesus as the suffering servant messiah because these disciples of Jesus are persecuted and ask: why is this happening to me? The gospel replies that the disciple is one who follows the master's path of faithful love, giving one's last breath as Jesus did.

Mark's gospel portrays the original disciples as fearful and very slow to learn that the servant of God must love even unto death, thus teaching the community that they, too, will receive Jesus' patient mercy as they struggle in faith, even as Peter and the earlier disciples did.

Luke's Gospel. Luke's community is a missionary church that is learning to expand its boundaries of sharing and concern. Only slowly and painfully are they realizing that life in Christ calls them to care for more than just their own family and friends. As Jesus was impelled by the Spirit to bring the good news of God's convenantal love to the poor and oppressed, so they are called to lives of complete generosity and service to all. Those in positions of authority are reminded, particularly, of their responsibility to follow Jesus' path of serving, not being served.

Matthew's Gospel. Matthew's community experiences its identity as deeply committed to Mosaic teaching with Jesus as *the* expositor, yet wrenched by outsiders challenging this identity. They long to clarify and reaffirm their bonds with Israel's tradition, law, and experience of righteousness. Their meditation, therefore, is upon Jesus, the personification of wisdom, whose interpretation of the law is the embodiment of Israel's righteousness: mercy, forgiveness, trust in the midst of persecution—the beatitudes. Living according to this teaching is to cooperate with God in bringing into being God's new covenant, that is, God's reign of peace and justice, in a community called *ekklesia*, "church."

John's Gospel. This community experiences unity as well as alienation. More than any other gospel community, its members realize the depth of Jesus' unity with God and their own indwelling in God through rebirth as God's daughters and sons, as friends and sisters/brothers of Jesus, as those in whom the new Paraclete lives and continues to teach the meaning of Jesus' words. Their alienation stems from being rejected by the wider Jewish community. This gospel reflects this situation and their need to respond to the challenges raised by this rejection.

At the heart of the apostolic spirituality of the fourth gospel is the experience of being sent even as Jesus was sent from the Father. Over and over this gospel echoes the phrase "as . . . me, so . . . you." In their own way the disciples experience the *same* relationship Jesus has to his Father, the same work as Jesus, the same Spirit, the same joy, the same life!

Spirituality of the Hebrew Bible. For Paul and the communities of the gospels, all understanding of their religious experience comes through interpretation of the Jewish scripture in light of their unique experience of Jesus, the Christ. Christians, valuing their Jewish roots, must respect the contemporary and continuing integrity of revelation in the Hebrew bible on its own terms. For this interpretation it is best to turn to Jewish theology. For example, Abraham J. Heschel's theology of God's *pathos* (1971) examines Israel's tradition regarding torah, prophets and wisdom from the perspective of its central religious experience: God's search for humanity.

Summary. In the biblical vision, spiritual maturity is deep and inclusive love. It is the loving relationship to God and others born of the struggle to discern where and how God is present in the community, in ministry, in suffering, in religious and political dissension, and in one's own sinfulness. Guidelines which help one "test the spirits" do not eliminate the need, ultimately, to trust one's own sense of vocation in the absence of certitude. Maturity is understood primarily as a matter of relationship. Yet the dimension of self-direction and adult freedom is also present in the language of a call to conversion and to fidelity in spiritual darkness.

B. Early Christianity

Liturgical and theological texts indicate that Christians understood their lives as personal participation in the mystery of Christ begun in faith, sealed by baptism into the death and resurrection of Jesus Christ, nourished by sharing in the Lord's supper which celebrated his saving presence and action in their lives, and expressed by universal love that bore witness to life in the Spirit and drew others to faith. This common faith was experienced within the diversity of the later Roman empire's history: persecution of Christians, and then rule by a Christian emperor; eastern and western centers of culture and theology; profound theological disputes; assimilation and rejection of the dominant culture.

Christian spirituality is composed of a constellation of elements (e.g., God-images, community, prayer, ministry, asceticism) that receive different emphases at various times or for different persons. Rearranging one element of the constellation affects all the others. Early Christian history exemplifies this principle. Francine Cardman (1978) notes, for example, that by centering on the Sunday eucharist celebrated in house churches or in larger communities made up of rich and poor, educated and illiterate, women and men, early Christian spirituality reinforced certain feelings, insights, and convictions. Love, acceptance, reconciliation, hope, and the challenge to honest love and generosity were dominant feelings. Understanding the various senses of scripture—literal, allegorical, moral, and eschatological—was fostered through informed preaching. Conviction deepened that community is the primary place where one meets the risen Lord.

Initial emphasis on martyrdom affected all later interpretation of Christian experience. Whereas Paul sees ministry as the imitation of Christ, early martyrs understand their experience as the closest imitation of Jesus. Praising martyrdom, then, reinforced Greek culture's tendency to deny the body and the world. When martyrdom was no longer possible, complete self-denial was sought in asceticism and early monasticism.

Asceticism arose as a counter-cultural movement against the Christian church that was too identified with Alexandrian, Antiochene, Byzantine and Roman institutions. Primarily a lay movement, it had two sides: solitary, that tended toward excessive contempt for the flesh, and communal, which stressed simple prayer that relished scripture and promoted the necessary attitudes for the interpretation of scripture: deep charity and purity of conscience. Some theologians (e.g. Augustine) lived in community precisely in order to foster their study and ministry of teaching. Wise ascetics (e.g. Benedict) attracted persons seeking spiritual guidance. Benedict's rule, and before him Basil's, set the tone for the monasticism (and its offspring mendicancy) of east and west.

Sayings of the desert fathers and mothers manifest a profound realization that tradition is not a set formula but a continuity of life lived according to the gospel. Desert wisdom is perennial, yet naturally mirrors the authoritarian, partriarchal and matriarchal society from which it comes.

Christian culture's absorption of ancient learning promoted an influential model and method of spirituality. Its ideal became philosophical contemplation which centered on the mind. Its method involved subjection of the passions to reason.

As Peter Brown explains (1985), the ideal of virginity, practiced by a small minority of women and men, enjoyed a moral and cultural supremacy in Christianity that was unchallenged until the reformation. For men and women in ancient Mediterranean society, sexual abstinence was a social act with negative and positive connotations foreign to modern post-puritans. For early Christians, virginity meant fighting against tensions of unfulfilled sexuality; but, even more significantly, it meant struggling against the force of social convention which swept a person into his or her "natural" social role as a married person, enjoying sexual intercourse in order to perpetuate family and kinship. Positively, in virginity one committed oneself to different grounds of social cohesion: to "true" joining out of free choice, in faith, in order to "mediate" between the divine and the human. This high theory was not always practiced, yet its symbolic power cannot be underestimated. Gradually, this theory modified the Platonic universe of soul withdrawn from body, so that the emphasis became one of the withdrawal of the body-self from society's claims regarding the primacy of family and kin. This made the inclusive gospel vision of society more possible if not more actual.

Summary. Spiritual maturity, in this era, continued to be envisioned as union with God and love of neighbor. Insertion into Antiochene, Alexandrian, Byzantine and Roman institutions caused these relationships to be evaluated against the ideals of charity and purity of conscience as well as those of contempt for the flesh and subjection of passion to reason. Virginity as an ideal not only prompted renunciation of sexuality but it also legitimated a kind of personal autonomy through rejection of social conventions regarding family.

C. Medieval Spirituality

This period was innovative, for example, in styles of religious life and art, but it was not revolutionary because it remained firmly rooted in traditions from the previous era.

Popular spirituality could be distinguished from professional. Mass conversions, low levels of general education, and
pastoral neglect promoted religious experience characterized
by a cult of relics, magic under the guise of sacraments, pilgrim-
ages simply for the sake of travel, and thinly veiled paganism.
Professional spirituality was informed by study and guidance.

Professional religious life flourished in a variety of forms
described in the research edited by Jill Raitt (1987). While
women and men continued to withdraw in solitude, there also
emerged an urban ministry of clerics devoted to including laity
in cathedral liturgy. Monks tended to see monastic life as the
only place in which the image of God could truly be restored
to humanity in this life. In contrast, there arose mendicant
women and men (e.g. Francis, Dominic) convinced that genuine evangelical life was possible outside the monastic structure.
Believing that anyone could preach who was called by God's
Spirit, they wandered the countryside calling all to conversion,
using metaphors appealing to the new merchant class. Living in
poverty, they alternated periods of solitude with preaching that
focused on the humanity of Jesus in the incarnation and passion.
The beguines were another type of lay group. Independent
from men's authority, these women often lived at home in vol-
untary poverty and chastity. With no formal church supervi-
sors, they combined work, common prayer, and life in the
world. Eventually these women were forced into the cloister
and mendicant preaching was clericalized.

The constellation of elements in medieval spirituality was
moved, for some, by the image of God and of Jesus as mother.
Although Julian of Norwich may be best known for her theology of God's motherhood, she is not original since feminine
God images are present in the Bible and in early Christian writing. The significance of her contribution must be evaluated in
light of the fact that the most developed theology of the motherhood of God and the nurturing qualities of Christ occurred in
the writing of medieval Cistercian monks. Thus, as an idea it
had more significance historically for men than for women.

Carolyn Walker Bynum's research (1984) demonstrates
that many Cistercian abbots, needing to supplement their expe-

rience of religious authority with what they considered feminine characteristics—gentleness, tenderness, availability—projected those qualities onto Christ, their model of monk and abbot. In the process of infusing authority with love, these men romanticized motherhood, repeated female stereotypes, and imaged Christ as a nursing mother even while they maintained their distance from and hostility toward actual women.

Medieval spirituality interprets its experience of being human as one of being the image and likeness of God. Here it continues patristic themes: grace as divinization, intellect, memory, and will as reflections of the Trinity (e.g. *The Cloud of Unknowing*), the image of God as given from the beginning yet tarnished by sin, and asceticism as the way to develop the true likeness to God (e.g. *The Imitation of Christ*). For medieval women and men, such as Clare and Francis of Assisi, for example, one becomes one's true self through conformity to the model of true humanity: Jesus Christ.

The rise of the cult of Mary is one of the most striking features of medieval spirituality, explains Elizabeth A. Johnson (1987). During this period the figure of Mary changed from the inspiring mother of Christ, to the merciful mother of the people, to the sovereign queen of heaven and earth who protected her faithful ones. At times her ability to rescue became the focus of devotion to the point where she functioned as an acting agent independent even of God. Feminist writers, such as Eleanor C. McLaughlin (1974), fault the medieval cult of the Virgin for creating an image of woman according to androcentric perceptions and needs, leaving the situation of real women unaffected by the glorification of this one woman.

In the midst of the wars and religious divisions of late western medieval history, significant women heeded the voices of their inner religious experience which urged them to redirect political affairs. Catherine of Siena, for example, advised the pope and Joan of Arc led armies. They demonstrate the inseparability of religious and "worldly" experience.

Eastern spirituality is well represented in Gregory of Palamas (1296–1359). He integrated *hesychasm*, eastern Christianity's ancient tradition of contemplative monasticism, into a doctrinal synthesis. In his anthropology, the whole person is called now to enjoy the first fruits of final deification. This includes social and political implications. In his theology of union with God, Gregory teaches that we participate in God's existence, God's "energies," yet God's essence remains unattainable and beyond all participation. Gregory wants to emphasize the immediacy and intimacy of the union while preserving the ultimate transcendence of God.

A central feature of *hesychasm* is prayer of the heart, that is, prayer of the whole person, including the body. Its aim is to be conscious of the grace of baptism that is already given but hidden by sin. Its method was influenced by Islam's joining of the holy name to the rhythm of breathing. Its wider context is the eastern understanding of active and contemplative life. These terms refer to interior development, not to external situation. Active refers to the redirection (not suppression) of passions, and contemplative refers to silence of heart. An enclosed nun, therefore, could be in the active life-stage while a doctor committed to her patients could be in the contemplative life if she had silence of heart. Prayer of the heart is a way of constant prayer possible to all persons, not just to monks or nuns.

Summary. Medieval spirituality envisioned spiritual maturity as wholehearted conformity to Christ's love and care for all, a care which was often imaged as motherly. New forms of religious life revealed that maturity could be attained outside monastic settings. Personal judgment was needed in order to discern the appropriate response to new forms of apostolic life and to be faithful to interior development understood as both active and contemplative.

D. The Reformation

Protestant experience of aspects of medieval tradition led to a new understanding of spirituality. Monasticism was no longer desirable as the special place to experience God; rather, God was free to be present intensely in all of life. Celibacy was no longer the privileged state of life in which to achieve union with God; instead, marriage was valued, and in some cases became almost an obligation for clergy. In this move women lost the advantages of convent life, among them independence from partriarchal marriage and the opportunity for higher education; instead they received a new role-expectation: the pastor's wife. Reformation Catholics and Protestants each tended to respond to issues by emphasizing the opposite position and assuming that the other's view had no merit. Contemporary Catholics, on the other hand, can appreciate Luther's insights and notice relationships to the great Spanish mystics that neither Luther nor Teresa and John consciously intended.

For Luther, speech about God is speech about absence; God is met only in the cross of Christ, that is, in lonely despair where there are no signs of transcendence, no conceptual neatness, no mystical assurances. Teresa of Jesus and John of the Cross would agree with Luther's conviction that one cannot contain or control God. Luther and authentic Catholic contemplative tradition object to the perversion of contemplation into a mysticism which imprisons God in a set of human experiences. John of the Cross, especially, teaches the inevitability of the dark night in which human desire is transformed and one's human projections onto God are eventually surrendered to allow authentic union with God in Christ. John, Teresa and Luther would agree also that knowledge of God is possible only on God's terms: when humans yield their self-assertive will and allow God to take the initiative in undeserved love. This affinity between Luther and the great Carmelite reformers does not, however, discount their differences regarding grace, church, and human nature.

Carmelite reform, initiated by Teresa of Jesus and extended to the friars through John of the Cross, intended to make religious life a community of loving friends, living in poverty and solitude in order to be completely disposed to God's action for the sake of the needs of the church. Teresa's astute interpretation of her own process of religious development, explained in her *Life* and *The Interior Castle* and other writings, eventually made her a doctor of prayer for the universal church. While describing years of struggle with her own personality and cultural conditioning in order to surrender to God,

Teresa communicates her experience of deepening prayer through the image of four waters. Her efforts at self-knowledge and honest love (drawing water from the well) yield a greater capacity for receiving God's love (a water wheel eases the effort); fidelity in the desert of love's purification allows the full force of God's acceptance and love to inundate her (the river) with unusual gifts of intimacy and leadership in the church (rain).

Ignatius of Loyola also distilled his religious experience into guidelines for spiritual growth. His *Spiritual Exercises* are an adaptable, imaginative method of meditation and contemplation of scripture designed to assimilate one to the mysteries of Christ and facilitate discernment as a contemplative in apostolic action.

Summary. Both Protestant and Catholic reformers envisioned maturity as surrender to God's free love in Christ and as fidelity to one's interior call. Religious upheaval and reform tended to reinforce the need for fidelity to one's conscience in the midst of uncertainty. Therefore, this era developed the themes of personal discernment and explicit self-knowledge.

E. Modern Spirituality

As the reformation affected later Catholic spirituality through Spanish writers, so from the seventeenth century onward French spirituality was very influential.

The seedbed was not so much monasteries or universities as the parlor of Madame Acarie, later known as the Carmelite Marie of the Incarnation. Her discussion group included Benedict of Canfield and Pierre de Berulle. They absorbed the Platonic perspective of Denys the Areopagite, a medieval writer incorrectly identified for centuries as a disciple of Paul, and reshaped it to support their own understanding of spirituality. Canfield's *Exercise of the Will of God* stressed holiness as accessible to all. Its central theme is the mysticism of "nothingness" by which a person experiences the self-emptying of Jesus Christ in his passion. Berulle also teaches participation in the mysteries of Christ. In his *Grandeurs de Jesus* the goal of Christian life is to reproduce on earth the adoration and servitude of Christ in heaven, as William M. Thompson (1980) has explained.

This era was also influenced by the exceptional personality of Francis de Sales. A bishop best known for his warmth and sensitivity as a spiritual director, his *Introduction to the Devout Life* is a classic treatment of laity's pursuit of holiness in everyday life. Through his friend Jeanne de Chantal, foundress of the Visitation Order, de Sales' theory and practice of spiritual direction became a lasting influence.

Jansenism, a complex and controversial combination of theological, political, and economic issues, was named for Cornelius Jansen whose rigorist presentation of Augustine's theology of grace had long-lasting effects. Jansen maintained that grace is irresistible; in confession a penitent should never be given the benefit of the doubt; one should sometimes give up holy communion as an act of devotion or through mortification; moral life must be strict. Although Blaise Pascal is associated with this movement, he is not Jansenist in any narrow sense.

Discovery of new lands generated a missionary spirituality characterized by the desire to announce the mystery of Christ as his ambassador by means of an evangelical life of fidelity and unswerving charity. Inspired by the mystique of Isaac Jogues and other missionary martyrs, it was encouraged by the pope's establishment of the Congregation for the Propagation of the Faith.

A distinct theological discipline called mystical theology also arose. Its aim was doctrinal and scientific study of the journey of the soul to contemplative union with God. All steps of the spiritual life were conceived as preparation for this union. Manuals of mystical theology attempted scientific classification of these steps, asking, for example, whether "spiritual marriage" is a state higher than "transforming union." This discipline offered a type of unified, speculative structure of all spirituality.

Nineteenth and twentieth century spirituality was, like all previous spirituality, creative response to God's presence discerned in events and ideas. Response to the enlightenment, secularism, atheism, and political revolution ranged from anti-intellectualism in theology and piety on the one hand, to redemptive identification with modern struggles of faith in Therese of Lisieux and attempts to reconcile science and religion in Pierre Teilhard de Chardin. Concern to restore biblical prayer, share monastic riches with the laity, and reunite spirituality and theology motivated the liturgical movement. Religious revival took the form of parish "missions" which paralleled Protestant methods of evangelization in some ways. Responses to industrialism included the social spirituality taught in papal encyclicals, Dorothy Day's spirituality of the Catholic Worker movement, and the founding of the Little Brothers and Sisters of Jesus who, inspired by Charles de Foucauld, live a ministry of evangelical presence as poor workers among workers. Devotion to Mary tended to compensate for Jansenist rigorism and partriarchal religion by promoting Mary as the kind, approachable mediatrix of all grace.

Summary. Modern spirituality continued to respond to ideas and events which opened new perspectives on faith and doubt, on mission, science, social structures, and world religions. Maturity remained a matter of loving relationships and fidelity to one's personal call and gifts. Radically new possibilities and re-examination of religious authority reinforced the need for discernment which demands that one both trust and evaluate personal decisions.

Theological and pastoral trends that shifted Catholic emphasis from "the soul" to the person, from dogma to history, from logic to method, from first principles to experience, as Bernard Lonergan noted (1974), culminated in the renewal of Vatican II.

II. Spirituality in the Life of the Church Since Vatican II

All the documents of Vatican II reflect concern for renewed spirituality. Some of their implications for the life of the church were expected while others were quite unanticipated.

The Constitution on the Sacred Liturgy announces that the primary goal of the entire council is to intensify Christian spirituality, that is, "the daily growth of Catholics in Christian living" (#1). This is the primary reason for renewing the liturgy, especially the eucharist. Enabling Christians to participate knowingly, actively, and fruitfully (#11) will draw them into authentic religious experience, namely conscious participation in the mysteries of Christ's life, ministry, death, and resurrection.

Dramatic consequences followed. Catholics shifted from an experience of going to watch "the priest say mass" in Latin to one of being drawn into an experience of active listening to scripture (Revelation #21) read in their own language, and responding in song, procession, antiphonal prayer, and participation in the eucharistic meal of unity, remembering Jesus' saving teaching and action. Personal faith became more demanding because this style of participation made it harder simply "to go through the motions" of attendance. In addition, renewed liturgy set up expectations that one would receive adequate understanding of scripture and a call to conversion, warm welcome from an inclusive community, and faithful witness to Jesus' ministry to the poor and marginalized. When these expectations were not met, Christians became dissatisfied and responded in various ways.

Post-Vatican II Catholicism has, for many reasons, become less and less a eucharistic community. Women's alienation from the liturgy's predominantly masculine God-language and male clericalism, for example, has caused some to turn away from the Roman Catholic eucharist. Availability of fewer priests and the lack of alternatives such as the ordination of women or married men has led to the phenomenon of thousands of Christian communities living far from the council's vision of the eucharist as the "outstanding means for Christians to express in their lives and manifest to others the mystery of Christ and the nature of the Church" (#1).

Two themes in the Dogmatic Constitution on the Church significantly affected spirituality: the universal call to holiness, and the call to the same holiness cultivated in various duties of life. First, "all the faithful of whatever rank . . . are called to the fullness of the Christian life and to the perfection of charity" (#40). Because the document continues to assume the traditional perspective of higher and lower "rank" in which bishops, priests, and religious were assumed to be called to a special holiness, this document, in effect, extended this same call to "ordinary lay people." They heard it and responded enthusiastically to grass roots movements for spiritual renewal such as cursillo, marriage encounter, and the charismatic movement. Emphasizing the council's biblical definition of holiness as mercy, kindness, humility, and other fruits of the Spirit, these movements often manifest an egalitarian style of ministry.

Although the documents of Vatican II retain the view of different ranks (e.g. clergy and laity) and states of life (lay and religious), the hierarchical attitude perpetuated by this language was undermined by also teaching that the "same holiness is cultivated in various duties of life" (Church #41), and the whole church "is missionary by her very nature" (Missions #2). Inspired by this more egalitarian vision, laity, sisters, brothers, and priests made a cursillo, for example, in which they both received and gave spiritual ministry, or joined a charismatic prayer group in which the Spirit's gifts of leadership were sometimes recognized in women rather than in priests.

The notion of every Christian participating in the church's "mission" was gradually translated into language of universal "ministry." Under the impact of returning to scripture as "the pure and perennial source of the spiritual life" (Revelation #21), Catholics discovered the New Testament experience of the ministry of reconciliation exercised by every person through mutually supportive gifts. Although the documents of Vatican II speak of "ministry" only when referring to the clergy, within twenty years the dominant practical understanding of "ministry" became one that is based upon the experience of spiritual gifts, not upon ordination to the priesthood. Moreover, there is widespread declericalization of ministries such as spiritual direction and retreats, areas once assumed to be the prerogative of priests.

Reversing a long tradition of viewing "the world" as inimical to the church, as a sphere divided from "the sacred" and to be converted and taught, the document on the Church in the

Modern World affirms the value of the world and confesses that the church could learn from the world and should be receptively reading "the signs of the times." Christian spirituality, therefore, becomes more authentically biblical, as it discerns God's presence in the midst of the events of history as well as in the movements of one's inner spirit.

Not only is the secular world affirmed as having something to teach the church, but also Protestants, eastern Orthodox, and non-Christian religions are approached with respectful attention to what they can contribute to Catholic spirituality. "Each branch of the human family possesses . . . some part of the spiritual treasure entrusted by God to humanity . . ." (Church in the Modern World #86). The church's task is to uncover, cherish, and ennoble all that is true, good, and beautiful in the human community (#96).

This openness to receive from persons outside the Catholic community encouraged not only unprecedented outreach in interreligious dialogue but also new openness to diversity within Catholic spirituality. Black, Mexican, Filippino, Puerto Rican and other cultures celebrate and develop their unique religious experience in liturgy, education, and action for justice. In some places in the United States they constitute the majority of Catholics, while in other places they are regarded as marginal because the New Testament principle of genuine diversity in unity is not yet familiar or acceptable to many Catholics. Openness to diversity and critical evaluation of the past has, in fact, created not only possibilities for enrichment and shared gifts but also divisiveness and polarity.

In summary, the perspective of Vatican II has generated a holistic spirituality which adheres to God at the center of everything and seeks to cooperate with God in bringing God's reign into every sphere of life, or, for some, a defensive spirituality that values certitude more than understanding.

Thomas Merton is a paradigm of spirituality in the life of the church of Vatican II. Long before the council, Merton gradually perceived the direction of God's Spirit in his life moving him from a desire to flee the world in order to find God in the sacred sphere of the monastery, to a realization that his former perspective was an illusion. "Finding God" was, rather, a matter of entering fully into himself and into every dimension of the world of human friendship, of action for justice, of humanity praising and seeking God in non-Christian religions. Catholic spirituality since Vatican II has moved steadily in these directions, rejoicing in the Spirit's gifts and facing the inevitable questions and discomfort associated with new pathways.

III. Issues in Spirituality Today

Spirituality today refers both to lived experience and to an academic discipline. The latter is past the initial stage in which scholars develop some common vocabulary, basic categories, and journals for publication. Yet it has not reached the mature point at which it has the generalized theory that would enable it to be a developed discipline fully recognized in academic circles. Spirituality is in the fascinating intermediate stage in which it creates its new identity while remaining linked to its family of origin.

A primary issue, then, is the nature of the discipline itself. This description from Sandra M. Schneiders (1986), director of doctoral studies in spirituality at the Graduate Theological Union, Berkeley, California, clarifies the term "spirituality," and the basic characteristics of the discipline.

Virtually everyone discussing sprituality today talks about self-transcendence in its philosophical or religious sense. The *philosophical meaning* of spirituality is based on a distinction between the material and the spiritual, the spiritual being understood as that capacity for self-transcendence through knowledge and love which characterizes the human being as a person. Thus, in the philosophical sense of the term, all humans are essentially "spiritual" and actualize that dimension of selfhood through the establishment of human relationships. The *religious meaning* of spirituality is based on the conception of what constitutes the proper and highest actualization of the human capacity for self-transcendence in personal relationships, namely, relationship with God. Spirituality, then, in its religious sense, refers to the relationship between the individual and God pursued in the life of faith, hope, and love. The *Christian meaning* is a particular specification of the religious meaning, indicating actualization of the capacity for self-transcendence that is constituted by the gift of the Holy Spirit which gives a relationship to God in Christ within the believing community. Christian spirituality, therefore, is trinitarian, christological, ecclesial religious experience.

When spirituality is understood as Schneiders suggests, certain features will characterize the emerging discipline which purports to study spirituality. First, this discipline will be *descriptive and analytic* rather than prescriptive and evaluative. Whether the researcher is studying discernment, action for social justice, God images or any of the hundreds of other topics which are attracting scholars today, the first task will be to understand the phenomenon on its own terms, that is, as it is or was actually experienced by Christians. Second, an *interdisciplinary approach* is essential. Very diverse phenomena fall within the field of spirituality and each demands its appropriate method. At times it may be historical, at other times it may be psychological or literary or theological. No single method is sufficient to deal with the documents, events, or persons that comprise the "data" of this field. Third, spirituality is now committed to an *ecumenical and even cross-cultural* approach. Part of understanding any phenomenon is seeing how it fits into the larger picture of the human quest for meaning and integration of which the Christian quest is only one actualization. Fourth, spirituality is *inclusive or holistic* in its approach. It is not "the soul" that seeks integration in holiness of life but the whole person, body and spirit, mind and will and emotions, individual and social, male and female. Fifth, spirituality seems to be a necessarily *"participant" discipline*. The researcher must know the spiritual quest by personal experience if he or she is to understand the phenomena of spirituality. One might be studying a spirituality quite different from one's own, but without some analogous experience one could hardly be expected to comprehend the activities and passivities of the spiritual life. Sixth, spirituality studies not principles to be applied nor general classes or typical cases but *concrete individuals:* persons, works, events. Consequently the researcher in spirituality is necessarily involved in what Ricoeur (1976) has called the "science of the individual" in which interpretation plays the key role and validation of interpretation through a dialectic of explanation and understanding rather than verification of repeatable scientific results is the objective. Lastly, spirituality, like psychology, has a *triple objective* that cannot be neatly simplified. One studies spirituality to understand it; but one also studies it in order to foster one's own spirituality and to foster the spirituality of others. The relative importance of each of these objectives differs from scholar to scholar and project to project but it is not possible to state once and for all that spirituality is either a theoretical or a practical discipline. It is both, although the emphasis varies at different moments in each project.

As I have elaborated elsewhere (1982), the methods and content of recent books and journals in spirituality demonstrate at least five significant trends in this field: sustained attention to feminist issues, concern for the link between prayer and social justice, reliance on classical sources for answers to current questions, recognition of the value of developmental psychology and its understanding of "the self," and agreement that experience is the most appropriate starting point.

The presence of one trend often includes several others, as Mary Jo Weaver's summary of feminist spirituality (1985, pp. 211–12) demonstrates. Feminist spirituality is both old and new, alive to ancient rhythms of the goddess while willing to experiment with spontaneous feminist rituals. It is rooted in the tradition—sometimes eager to claim connections with the eucharistic celebration of the Christian church—and yet opposed to its expression of exclusive male power. Roman Catholic feminist sprituality is clearly political, in the sense that it is predicated on a worldview that finds the sacred in what used to be called the secular, and yet may have something much in common with mystical prayer: perhaps God/ess (Rosemary R. Ruether's term for the fullness of divinity, combining masculine and feminine words for the divine) can only be experienced in a combination of active service on behalf of the marginalized and lively, daring participation in moments of divine disclosure deep within the soul.

Roman Catholic feminist spirituality, Weaver maintains, recapitulates the questions of feminist historians by interrogating the tradition of female sanctity in Catholicism. By an exclusive focus on Teresa of Avila as a mystic without corresponding attention to her uphill struggle for personal integration and power the tradition obscured an important part of her value for feminist interpreters. Similarly, past visions of female sanctity emphasized Catherine of Siena's obedience to the pope or disparagement of female weakness to the neglect of her independence and personal power as a reformer and spiritual director. By choosing to look differently at these saints, feminist researchers remind us that nuns and laywomen have always encountered opposition in the church when they embodied visions that were at odds with the option of complementarity (i.e. women complete men by serving and supporting their roles) and cloister presented to them by partriarchal males allegedly speaking for God. In looking at Julian of Norwich, we are reminded of how much we need feminist theologians and critical interpreters of the tradition in addition to visionaries. Most of all, in gathering the many versions of Mary together to intuit the possibilities of a composite symbol, feminists convey some sense of the need for solidarity and the power of collective action.

In short, Weaver's summary of feminist spirituality exemplifies the five themes mentioned above. She assumes the importance of classical sources and a starting point in experience as well as the centrality of the issues of self-development and social justice.

The issue of "the self" is the focal issue in contemporary spirituality's examination of the relationship between psychology and religion and between grace and nature. Because this theme is central to this book, the rest of the chapter will examine Thomas Merton's interpretation of the classical spiritual tradition of the "true self" in light of modern psychological concern for maturity.

Contemplation, for Merton (1962), fulfills our deepest human capacities, yet it does not come without some work on our part. We must develop certain human intellectual and affective capacities in order to facilitate contemplation. For example, reason must sift critically all spiritual experiences in order to judge which ones really correspond to genuine faith. Imagination, originality, freshness of response—qualities dulled by industrial society—need to be reinvigorated in order to promote contemplative experience. Most of all, one must "return to the heart," to love, to one's deepest center which includes and goes far beyond the consciousness reached by studies in psychology. For contemplation, in Merton's eyes, is life itself, fully awake to oneness with God. The intuition of our "real self" brings this awareness of profound union with God and with all persons and things.

Merton's model of spiritual development, as William Shannon (1981) notes, is basically a pattern of discovery. As we discover our true self we also discover the true God on whom we depend, and this discovery is a matter of choices, of ever greater freedom, and of awareness or discernment. All of these are interdependent. Merton—true to the contemporary discipline of spirituality which begins by examining concrete individual experience through a "participant" mode—describes the process in first person terms. I discover my true self by conscious choices to love, by choices which deliver me from self-seeking. This deliverance is the core of freedom, because the most important aspect of freedom is the liberation from whatever tends to keep alive the illusion (the false self) that opposes God's reality living in me. As long as I perceive no greater subjective reality in me than my false self, I have no freedom. When I am delivered from self-seeking, then I am free to seek God on whom I am dependent and who is present at the heart of my true self. My discovery or knowledge of God is paradoxically a knowledge not of God as the object of scrutiny, but of myself as utterly dependent on God's saving and merciful knowledge of me. Ultimately, Merton declares, you discover there is no duality between your true self and God. To a friend Merton once confided, "You have to see your will and God's will dualistically for a long time. You have to experience duality for a long time until you see it's not there."

Although Merton, a contemplative monk, views the self primarily from a theological point of view his discussion necessarily has implications for psychological issues. For example, the "true self" is a reality below the level of ego consciousness, but this does not make ego consciousness irrelevant. The ego contributes to contemplation by actively opening to deeper levels of awareness and by facing the fact that it is an illusion to consider itself the whole self. Typical of Catholic theology of nature and grace, Merton views the self as innately, naturally self-transcending and would, therefore, expect to find evidence of transcendence in psychological theories of the self. On the other side of the issue, psychologically sophisticated study of Merton's spirituality of the self can serve as the basis for a theology of ongoing conversion, as Walter E. Conn (1986) has demonstrated.

Other aspects of this issue of the self will, no doubt, constitute the agenda for spirituality in the future. As scholars examine the implications of psychoanalysis, for example respondents to the research of W.W. Meissner (1984), they are asking how God-representations formed at early stages of development can be revised at more mature stages. As feminists, such as Jean Baker Miller (1976), question the validity of psychological models based on exclusively male observations of mother/child relationships they ask whether that relationship is more accurately described as mutuality rather than as fusion or mirroring understood only as receptivity. Responses to these questions could make a significant difference for understanding the nature of religious experience.

The agenda for spirituality also includes very practical sides of this issue of the self. For example, could a more adequate theory of the self resolve the tension some Christians experience between contemplative solitude and social service? Spirituality must also address the dangers of inviting people who have a formless or poorly differentiated self to simplify their prayer or devote themselves to religious ministry. Without explicit attention to the work of identity formation, in the former case, what is an inner condition of lack can be mistaken for the boundlessness of mystical union; in the latter case, a person might fuse with the ideology of a worthy cause and become authoritarian or a religious fanatic.

In summary, a synthesis of these trends sets the future agenda for Christian spirituality: a discipline that is rooted in experience, attentive to the issue of the self, nourished by history, and concerned for mutuality and equality of women and men. It is to these issues that we now turn in search of a model of human maturity that correlates with mature Christian spirituality.

References

Bouyer, Louis, Jean Leclercq, and Francois Vandenbroucke. *A History of Christian Spirituality.* 3 Vols. New York: Seabury, 1977, 1982.

Brown, Peter. "The Notion of Virginity in the Early Church." In *Christian Spirituality: Origins to the Twelfth Century,* edited by Bernard McGinn and John Meyendorf. New York: Crossroad, 1985.

Bynum, Carolyn Walker. *Jesus as Mother.* Berkeley: University of California, 1984.

Cardman, Francine. "A Lightening Look at the History of Christian Spirituality." In *The Wind Is Rising,* edited by William Callahan and Francine Cardman. Mt. Ranier, MD: Quixote Center, 1978.

Conn, Joann Wolski. "Horizons on Contemporary Spirituality." *Horizons* 9/1 (Spring 1982), 60–73.

Conn, Walter E. *Christian Conversion.* New York: Paulist, 1986.

Heschel, Abraham J. *The Prophets 2.* New York: Harper Torchbooks, 1971.

Johnson, Elizabeth A. "Marian Devotion in the Western Church." In *Christian Spirituality: High Middle Ages and Reformation,* edited by Jill Raitt. New York: Crossroad, 1987.

Lonergan, Bernard J.F. "The Future of Thomism." In his *Second Collection.* London: Darton, Longman & Todd, 1974.

McGinn, Bernard, John Meyendorff, and Jean Leclercq. *Christian Spirituality: Origins to the Twelfth Century.* New York: Crossroad, 1985.

McLaughlin, Eleanor Commo. "Equality of Souls, Inequality of Sexes: Woman in Medieval Theology." In *Religion and Sexism,* edited by Rosemary Radford Ruether. New York: Simon & Schuster, 1974.

W.W. Meissner, S.J., M.D. *Psychoanalysis and Religious Experience.* New Haven: Yale University Press, 1984. See also the Review Symposium on Meissner's book in *Horizons* 13/2 (Fall 1986), 389–410.

Merton, Thomas. *New Seeds of Contemplation.* New York: New Directions Books, 1962.

Miller, Jean Baker. *Toward a New Psychology of Women.* Boston: Beacon, 1976; and "The Development of Women's Sense of Self." Wellesley, MA: Stone Center Working Papers Series, 1984.

Raitt, Jill. ed. *Christian Spirituality: High Middle Ages and Reformation.* New York: Crossroad, 1987.

Ricoeur, Paul. *Interpretation Theory: Discourse and the Surplus of Meaning.* Fort Worth: Texas Christian University Press, 1976.

Schneiders, Sandra M. "Theology and Spirituality: Strangers, Rivals, or Partners?" *Horizons* 13/2 (Fall 1986), 253–274.

Shannon, William H. *Thomas Merton's Dark Path.* New York: Farrar, Straus and Giroux, 1981.

Thompson, William M. "A Study of Berulle's Christic Spirituality." In his *Jesus Lord and Savior.* New York: Paulist, 1980.

Weaver, Mary Jo. *New Catholic Women.* San Francisco: Harper & Row, 1985.

Williams, Rowan. *Christian Spirituality: A Theological History from the New Testament to Luther and St. John of the Cross.* Atlanta, GA: John Knox, 1980.

Chapter 2

An Alternative Position: Carol Gilligan

Carol Gilligan's book *In a Different Voice* (1982) is one of the most quoted psychology books of recent times. It has captured public attention because it boldly rejects the dominant model of human development which assumes that maturity is autonomy. Instead Gilligan offers a controversial alternative which equates maturity with relationship.

Since Christian spirituality also correlates maturity with relationship, perhaps Gilligan's model would be most compatible with it. In order to test this hypothesis and thus evaluate the suitability of Gilligan's new model for use in pastoral counseling and spiritual direction, this chapter will proceed in two steps. First, it will present Gilligan's central thesis, noting her own cautionary remarks concerning her claim about women's psychology. Second, her critics will speak, followed immediately by Gilligan's response. This will permit Gilligan to reinforce her basic conclusions and allow her critics' unanswered questions to remain as topics for our reflection. Our concern is whether the limitations of Gilligan's model restrict its suitability as a model to correlate with Christian maturity.

In a Different Voice

In 1977 Gilligan began to notice that none of the prevalent theories of adult development could take account adequately of the women's experience she found in her research. She later wrote *In a Different Voice* (1982) as an attempt to discover what was missed by the practice of leaving out girls and women from the research samples used to build these theories. In other words, she asked whether Piaget's and Kohlberg's descriptions of moral development, Erikson's description of identity development, Offer's description of adolescent development, and Levinson's and Vaillant's description of adult development, as well as more general accounts of human personality and motivation, contained a consistent conceptual and observational bias, reflected in their choice of all-male research samples. Her answer to the question of what is missing is this claim (hypothesis, in scientific research language): there is a different way of constituting the idea of the self and the idea of what is moral, different from the one most accounts of adult development consider normative. Gilligan sees in women's thinking the lines of a different conception of self and morality; she hears a different voice grounded in different images of relationship and implying a different framework for interpretation of moral issues.

The different voice, Gilligan cautions her readers, is characterized not by gender but by theme (1982, p. 2). Its association with women is an empirical observation, and its development is traced in the book primarily through women's voices. This association, however, is not absolute and the contrasts between male and female voices are presented in order to highlight a distinction between two modes of thought and to focus a problem of interpretation rather than to represent a generalization about either sex. No claims are made about the origins of the differences described or their distribution in a wider population, across cultures, or through time. Nevertheless, Gilligan is quick to point out that these differences clearly arise in a social context where factors of social status and power combine with reproductive biology to shape the experience of males and females and the relations between the sexes.

A central assumption underlies the research: the way people talk about their lives is significant; the language they use and the connections they make reveal the world that they see and in which they act. Consequently, Gilligan's study relies primarily on personal interviews and uses examples from literature, history, and philosophy to illustrate conclusions drawn from these interviews. In the three studies which form the basis of her conclusions, Gilligan asked the same set of questions about self and morality, and about experiences of conflict and choice. One study interviewed twenty-five college students. In another study Gilligan spoke to twenty-nine pregnant women ranging in age from fifteen to thirty-three at a time when they were considering a decision for abortion. In a third study Gilligan interviewed a sample of males and females matched for age, intelligence, education, occupation and social class at nine points across the life cycle from ages six to sixty.

In six chapters, Gilligan pursues one goal: to expand the understanding of human development by using the group left out in the construction of the prevailing theory in order to call attention to what is missing in its account. Seen in this light, the inability of most theories to account adequately for women's experience should not result in judging women as deficient but, rather, should provide a basis upon which to generate new theory. Potentially, this theory will yield a more encompassing view of the lives of both women and men.

Gilligan's argument begins with her thesis that the principal exponents of developmental theory (e.g. Freud, Erikson, Piaget, Kohlberg) take a perspective which makes male experience normative and interpret the differences manifest in female experience as irrelevant or deficient. For example, Erikson observes that for men the life-task of identity precedes that of intimacy and generativity, while for women these tasks seem instead to be joined. Intimacy goes along with identity, as the female knows herself and is known through relationships. Despite his observations about women, Erikson charts his life-cycle stages according to the male pattern. Regarding moral development, for another example, when women (who voice their judgments in terms of care and responsibility) and men (who use the language of rights and non-interference with others) are measured according to Kohlberg's theory of moral maturity, women usually are judged to be in stage three while men are in stage four. In general, women's psychology has consistently been described as distinctive in its greater orientation toward relationships and interdependence, while the generally accepted theories of development describe maturity as movement toward individuation and autonomy. Whereas much of psychology casts this situation as a "problem in women's development," Gilligan believes the problem is in the theory itself.

Gilligan cites Nancy Chodorow's work, *The Reproduction of Mothering* (1978), as a more adequate description of the situation of women and men. According to Chodorow, interpersonal dynamics are different for boys and girls (men and women) because women, universally, are more responsible for early child care. Girls, in forming their identity as female, experience themselves as like their mother, thus fusing the experience of attachment with the process of identity formation. In contrast, boys, in defining themselves as masculine, separate their mothers from themselves, thus curtailing their primary love and sense of empathic tie. Male development, therefore, is more emphatic about separateness of ego boundaries and female development gives privileged place to connection.

As a result of Gilligan's attention to both women's and men's experience, she judges that, according to the dominant psychological tradition, woman's place in man's life cycle is a place of guardianship for human values that are neglected or undervalued. Women, for example, recognize the continuing importance of attachment in the human life-cycle, and protect this recognition, while the dominant tradition celebrates separation and values autonomy. Gilligan does not conclude that we should praise women who value what is better than what men value. Rather, she desires a more encompassing life-cycle theory which would include "the different voice" not yet heard with equal attention in the dominant tradition.

Having noted that attachment is a central theme in "the different voice" revealed by women, Gilligan then examines men's and women's fantasies about relationships. Images of hierarchy are prominent in men's accounts, and women focus on web-images (p. 62). These two images convey different ways of structuring relationships and are associated with different views of self and morality. They pose a problem for men and women trying to understand each other because each image distorts the other's representation. For example, as the top of the hierarchy becomes the edge of the web, and as the center of a network of connection becomes the middle of a hierarchical progression, the place which the one image (person) marks as safe is seen as dangerous by the other person. These images also influence different modes of assertion and response. For example, while one would wish to be alone at the top and fears that others would get too close, the other would wish to be at the center of connection and would respond with fear if threatened with being too far out at the edge. These fears of being stranded or being caught in turn give rise to different images of affiliation and achievement (e.g. marriage as a "trap" or promotion as alienation from peers), and lead to different ways of acting and different ways of evaluating the consequences of choice.

Gilligan's interviews with women who are involved in a choice for or against abortion reveal these women's concepts of self and morality. She hears these women using a distinct moral language of selfishness and responsibility; indeed, it defines the moral problem as one of obligation to exercise care and avoid hurt. Inflicting hurt is considered selfish and immoral in its reflection of unconcern, while care is seen as the fulfillment of moral responsibility. The women's moral orientation, reflected in the repeated use of the words *selfish* and *responsible*, sets them apart, according to Gilligan, from the men whom Kohlberg studied and indicates these women's different understanding of moral development.

Three moral perspectives are revealed in these abortion decision interviews. They manifest a sequence of development of care which Gilligan believes (pp. 72–74) parallels Kohlberg's influential distinction between "preconventional," "conventional," and "postconventional" stages of development. Preconventional moral judgment is egocentric and derives moral constructs from individual needs (e.g. avoid punishment, receive reward). Conventional judgment is based on the shared norms and values that sustain relationships, groups, communities, societies (e.g. family, church, state). Postconventional judgment adopts a reflective perspective on societal values and constructs moral principles that are universal in application (e.g. justice). According to Gilligan, the "different voice" of an ethic of care begins development by caring for the self in order to ensure survival. This is followed by a transitional phase in which this judgment is criticized as selfish. Here the woman acquires a second perspective in which care is equated with goodness, and goodness is identified with self-sacrifice and conventional understandings of feminine roles of care-taking. Dawning awareness of the inequality of women perpetuated by this conventional position leads to a third position. It is concerned not with goodness but with truth or honesty. In this third position, a woman considers it responsible to extend care to her own needs, accounting herself equally possessing rights and deserving of care along with those others upon whom she has previously bestowed her ethic of caring.

At this point Gilligan cautions readers about generalizing from the data presented in the study of abortion-decisions, and she reinforces the need for her colleagues to examine real-life crises, such as abortion-decisions, when they are engaged in research on human development (p. 126). Gilligan's conclusions about the ethic of care were taken from a small, non-scientifically selected sample. In order to refine and validate the sequence mentioned above, additional longitudinal studies of women's moral judgments are needed. In addition, studies of people's thinking about other real dilemmas are needed in order to clarify the special features of the abortion choice. For example, a respondent to Gilligan's work suggested in *Signs* (1986, p. 306) that a comparable study be done by interviewing men making decisions regarding conscientious objection to joining the military. Here, as in the abortion decision, we might also hear anguished consideration of responsibility to families and care for family needs.

The essence of this developmental approach is that "crisis creates character." Evidence of changes described in women's thinking about responsibility and relationships suggests that the capacity for care and responsibility evolves through a coherent sequence of crises. These turning points evolve around the intersection of feelings and thoughts with disconcerting events (e.g. exploitive relationship, unexpected pregnancy) in the history of the women's lives (pp. 127–128).

Gilligan continues her argument for including "a different

voice" in developmental theory by proposing another thesis: changes in women's rights change women's moral judgments (p. 149). Among college students in the 1970s, for example, the concept of rights entered women's thinking to challenge the morality of self-sacrifice and self-abnegation, as when students would question the stoicism of a wife's assuming that she should deny herself graduate education or a personal career in order to take care of all parenting duties. Women replaced the illusion that these choices for parenting were innocent of detrimental consequences for their children or their marriage. They were replaced with an awareness that different choices were both possible and legitimate. Women struggled to grasp the essential notion of rights: that the interests of the self can be considered legitimate. This essential concept of rights changed women's conceptions of self by allowing them to see themselves as entitled to consider directly their own needs. When asserting themselves no longer seemed dangerous, one effect was to change the women's concept of relationship. It shifted from being a bond of continuing dependence to become a dynamic of interdependence. This, in turn, changed women's moral judgments. For example, the notion of care expanded from the paralyzing injunction not to hurt others into an injunction to act responsibly toward self and others and thus to sustain connection. Consciousness of the dynamics of human relationships could then become central to moral understanding. For example, a woman who is struggling to combine career and family might notice how her morality involves dilemmas about which action will sustain family relationships. On the one hand her career might improve father/child relationships by requiring her husband to share parenting tasks; on the other hand, working might require her to move away from important friendships and links with her own parents. Gilligan's point is that changes in women's rights change women's moral judgments by enabling women to consider it moral to care not only for others but for themselves.

Gilligan concludes her argument by insisting that the dominant psychological model of adulthood, which aims primarily at autonomy, should be replaced by a more complex rendition of human experience (p. 174). That is, the more appropriate norm of adult maturity is one which sees the truth of both attachment and separation in the lives of women and men and recognizes how these truths are carried by different modes of language and thought.

In this representation of maturity, the ethics of justice and those of care converge in the realization that just as inequality adversely affects both parties in an unequal relationship, so too passivity or not caring is destructive for everyone involved. This dialogue between justice (fairness) and care not only provides a better understanding of relations between the sexes but also gives rise to a more comprehensive portrayal of adult work and family relationships.

Critique and Gilligan's Response

Gilligan's critics, such as those in the forum published in *Signs* (1986, pp. 304–333), acknowledge that her work makes important contributions. They single out her efforts to criticize academic research based on men's experience alone and her redefinition of social vocabulary. They praise her elegant style and the historical and philosophical depth of her writing. In addition, they respect her attempts to demonstrate how gender is a social construction. Their criticism of her research deals primarily with three areas: method, interpretation, and implications for education. To date, she has responded to some of these criticisms but not to all.

Regarding method, Gilligan's critics point to the small number of studies cited and ask whether she has not oversimplified the case on differences between women and men and overinterpreted the meager data. In response, Gilligan (1986, p. 330) cites studies completed after the publication of her book which, she claims, confirm and refine the "different voice" hypothesis by demonstrating: (1) the justice and care perspectives are distinct orientations that organize people's thinking about moral problems in different ways; (2) boys and men who resemble those most studied by developmental psychologists tend to define and resolve moral problems within the justice framework, although they introduce considerations of care; (3) the focus on care in moral reasoning, although not characteristic of all women, is essentially a female phenomenon in the advantaged populations that have been studied.

Regarding interpretation of the data, Gilligan's critics in *Signs* (1986, pp. 306–309) notice that she does not explore the psychological limitations of the female "voice" which she identifies. They claim that the effect of Gilligan's argument is to encourage the conclusion that women really are more nurturant, less likely to dominate, and more likely to negotiate than are men. Gilligan's critics also claim that because her positive interpretation of the voice of care neglects to give equal attention to its possible detrimental effects on others, it runs two risks. First, there are the dangers of feminist self-righteousness and romantic oversimplification. Historically, the rhetoric of feminism which claimed that women would vote for peace and justice for all was later sobered by the evidence that women voted as the interests of their race and class dictated. Second, Gilligan, by emphasizing the biological basis of distinctive behavior (departing here from Chodorow, who emphasizes learning), permits her readers to conclude that women's alleged affinity for "relationships of care" is both biologically natural and a good thing. Gilligan's critics ask: How does her theory deal with the self-interest, selfishness, and meanness of spirit which women surely display as much as men?

Regarding the limitations of the female "voice," Gilligan responds (1986, p. 332) by noting only the way an ethic of care might be turned against women themselves. Her studies of women, she claims, locate the problem in female development neither in the values of care and connection nor in the relational definition of self, but in the tendency for women, in the name of virtue, to give care only to others and to consider it "selfish" to care for themselves.

Another significant problem is raised by Paul Philibert (1987) who is sympathetic to Gilligan's project and therefore troubled when she abandons in her book (1982) the well-founded position she adopted in an earlier article (1980). Having introduced the work of Perry (1968) into her analysis of the defects of Kohlberg's stages, Gilligan (1980) ended up with the proposal that moral education needs to describe two kinds of adult morality: a postconventional formal ethic (as in Kohlberg) and a postconventional contextual ethic (as in Perry). Building on Perry's description of the way persons enter a new world of moral experience through sustained conversation that criticizes and explores meanings and values, Gilligan concluded that her own research with women found that maturity was characterized by the mutual co-establishment of values through ongoing, committed conversation. In a comparison of the article just mentioned and Gilligan's book, Philibert is struck by the fact that Gilligan later abandoned in her book all evidence of what might be called consensual procedures. That is, in no instance do the interviews given in the book include a discussion of actual conversations between aggrieved or cooperating partners. In the final analysis, then, Gilligan's account of her contextual ethics of care falls prey to the same weakness that she attributes to Kohlberg's stage theory. Namely, it is a psychology of morality based upon individualistic, non-dialectical reflection. If, with Kohlberg, there is a morality of rights without effective cooperation (Gilligan's evaluation), with Gilligan there is a morality of care without effective co-construction (Philibert's evaluation). The failure to include that dimension in her moral analysis, despite her important witness to the factor of relationship in female moral imagination is, to Philibert's mind, a significant frustration of her project. To date, Gilligan has not yet responded to this criticism.

Gilligan shares with her critics a concern about the education of women and men. When presenting research about conflicts between achievement and care, Gilligan maintains, it is important that women's concerns not be labeled a sign of weakness, because this only reinforces the impression that women's apprehension in this area is groundless. Certainly, women need to engage the problems created by the overload of work and family because these conflicts fall most heavily on women. It is a disservice to both women and men, however, to imply that these are only women's problems. On another topic, it may be of particular interest at this time, Gilligan remarks, for both sexes to explore whether women's experience illuminates the psychology of non-violent strategies for resolving conflicts. The goal is to be as attentive to women's experience as the tradition of psychology has been to men's perspective so that a more inclusive theory might assist everyone's reflection upon the meaning of maturity.

Conclusions

Having synthesized Gilligan's position and noted her principal contributions to a comprehensive theory of development, I find her model of maturity not yet appropriate for use in pastoral counseling and spiritual direction. Although Gilligan's vision of maturity is better than most others, her projected goal of a more comprehensive view of both women's and men's lives is marred by four inadequacies.

(1) Gilligan concentrates on attachment only as it appears in women's lives and does not yet give equal attention to the way attachment functions in men's experience. Neither does she sufficiently connect the developmental issue of attachment in women to the opposite desire: for independence and autonomy. Gilligan's own theory, therefore, cannot yet account adequately for the full range of women's and men's experience.

(2) So far, Gilligan has explored only one negative aspect of women's penchant for attachment: the way that an ethic of care might be turned against women themselves, leading them to neglect their own legitimate needs in the name of self-sacrifice (1986, p. 332). Gilligan's position cannot yet account for the way an ethic of care does not preclude women displaying genuine selfishness and meanness of spirit toward others.

(3) Gilligan sees no problem in the relational definition of self which is so characteristic of women (1986, p. 332). Here Gilligan follows Jean Baker Miller (1976) who suggests guidelines for a new psychology of women based on women's way of constructing a self known always through mediation of care to others. Other feminist psychologists (M. Greenspan, 1983; L.

Eichelberger and S. Orbach, 1983) disagree and find in their practice of therapy evidence of problems for women when they construct the meaning of themself entirely through relationship. In these cases, women *are* relationships rather than have perspective on relationship. Consequently, these women often manifest problems such as an inability to see when relationships are becoming destructive to them. Gilligan's model of self cannot adequately account for this difficulty.

(4) Finally, as Philibert points out, Gilligan's theory does not yet sufficiently situate women's formation of an ethic of care within the wider social context in which women negotiate values. This context might promote women's positive values and contradict the tendencies which turn women against themselves.

A more adequate model of maturity has come from a colleague of Gilligan's at Harvard, Robert Kegan, who explicitly praises Gilligan's work and has constructed a developmental theory (1982) which intentionally avoids the inadequacies that have been explained above as problems with Gilligan's theory.

References

Chodorow, Nancy. *The Reproduction of Mothering.* Berkeley, CA: University of California Press, 1978.

Eichenbaum, Luise & Orbach, Susie. *Understanding Women: A Feminist Psychoanalytic Approach.* New York: Basic Books, 1983.

Gilligan, Carol. *In a Different Voice.* Cambridge, MA: Harvard University Press, 1982.

———— and Belenky, Mary F. "A Naturalistic Study of Abortion Decisions." In R. Selman and R. Yando, eds., *Clinical-Developmental Psychology.* New Directions for Child Development, no. 7. San Francisco: Jossey-Bass, 1980.

Greenspan, Miriam. *A New Approach to Women & Therapy.* New York: McGraw-Hill, 1983.

Kegan, Robert. *The Evolving Self: Problem and Process in Human Development.* Cambridge, MA: Harvard University Press, 1982.

Kerber, Linda K.; Greeno, Catherine G. and Maccoby, Eleanor
    E.; Luria, Zella; Stack, Carol B.; and Gilligan, Carol. "On
    In a Different Voice: An Interdisciplinary Forum." *Signs*
    11/2 (Winter 1986), 304–333.
Miller, Jean Baker. *Toward a New Psychology of Women.* Bos-
    ton: Beacon, 1976.
Perry, William. *Forms of Intellectual and Ethical Development
    in the College Years* New York: Holt, Rinehart and Win-
    ston, 1968.
Philibert, Paul. "Relation, Consensus, and Commitment as
    Foundations of Moral Growth." *New Ideas in Psychology* 5/
    2 (1987), 183–195.

Chapter 3

Comprehensive Development: Robert Kegan

Robert Kegan has developed a model of human maturity that is more helpful for pastoral counseling and spiritual direction than the one presented in Carol Gilligan's *In a Different Voice*. First, where Gilligan concentrates on attachment only in women's lives, Kegan pays attention to the way it functions for both women and men. And Kegan, unlike Gilligan, always examines attachment in relationship to its opposite desire: for independence and autonomy. His theory, therefore, can account more adequately for the full range of women's and men's experience. Second, where Gilligan explores only one negative aspect of women's affinity for attachment (i.e. that it makes them vulnerable to outside manipulation), Kegan is more comprehensive by examining the advantages and limitations of both attachment and autonomy as they occur within a comprehensive theory of lifespan development. Third, where *In a Different Voice* omits explicit attention to the wider social context in which women negotiate values, Kegan's theory of development includes, at every phase, attention to the social context in which the meaning of oneself and others is negotiated and renegotiated.

This chapter will concentrate on the practical application of Kegan's theory to situations in pastoral counseling. Later chapters will extend its application to include spiritual direction and then correlate these two aspects of pastoral care. First, however, is a brief summary of Kegan's view of maturity and the process through which one may attain it. Next is an outline of the social context of development. Everyone is always embedded in a culture that has three therapeutic functions: confirmation (holding on), contradiction (letting go), and continuity (staying put for reintegration at a more mature stage).

Finally, the chapter examines a case-study. All of this is presented in order to assist counselors and spiritual directors in their primary tasks: conveying to the client or spiritual friend an understanding of her or his experience *as she or he experiences it,* and presenting opportunities to move from a less to a more mature balance of relationship and autonomy—in other words, presenting therapeutic, redemptive possibilities.

The Evolving Self

In *The Evolving Self: Problem and Process in Human Development* (1982) Robert Kegan, of Harvard University and the Massachusetts School of Professional Psychology, presents his understanding of human development as meaning-making activity. This meaning-making is not only the unifying, but also the generating context for both thought and feeling, as well as for self and other (subject and object). Emotion, in this perspective, is the experience of the motion of defending, surrendering, and reconstructing a center of meaning. Evolutionary activity involves the very creating of the other (differentiation) as well as our relating to it (integration). Self-other relations emerge out of a lifelong process of development: a succession of more adequate differentiations of the self from the world in which it is embedded, each differentiation creating a more complex object of relation. Maturity in each phase of the process is a relative triumph of "relationship to" rather than "embeddedness in."

Psychoanalytic theory looks to infancy for its basic themes and categories. Kegan, on the other hand, in his constructive-developmental view (1982, p. 77), regards infancy as qualitatively no different from any other moment in the lifespan. What is fundamental is the activity of meaning-making evolution. The distinctive features of infancy (fusion, differentiation, belonging) are to be understood in the context of the same activity which is necessary throughout a person's life. Recurrence of these distinctive features in new forms later on in development are not seen as later manifestations of infancy issues, but contemporary manifestations of making-the-meaning-of "self" and "other," just as infancy issues are, in their own time, manifestations of meaning-making. For example, a sixteen year old boy who clings to his stepmother is not seen as immaturely regressing to childhood behavior but understood as experiencing the discomfort of the motion of surrendering a self that *is* a relationship to her, rather than *has* that relationship. At sixteen, his developmental process includes the strengths gained from earlier struggles with these issues; therefore he is not simply repeating the identical meaning-making of childhood. Helping him to see his behavior this way, rather than as embarrassingly childish, can offer opportunities for greater maturity.

Developmental Phases

Kegan explains five developmental phases or stages which may describe—but not necessarily be—every person's life history (1982, pp. 85–110). Each stage involves a certain kind of balance between differentiation and integration, between the universal human longing for both autonomy and inclusion. Each balance is a temporary solution to the lifelong tension between the yearnings for inclusion and distinctness. Each balance resolves the tension in a different way. At one phase the balance will tip slightly in favor of autonomy, while at the next stage it will favor inclusion.

(1) Infancy is a transition from complete incorporation in the parent into the *impulsive* balance (stage one) of a two year old. This transformation occurs through a process that is repeated: decentration, emergence from embeddedness. Gradually the infant ceases being her reflexes and, instead, has them. In disembedding herself from her reflexes the two year old comes to have reflexes rather than be them. The new self is now embedded in impulses or wishes, in that which coordinates the reflexes. The new self is "hatched out" through a process of differentiation from that which was the very subject of personal organization and which now becomes the object of a new subjectivity which coordinates it. In this impulsive balance the

meaning of the self *is* its impulses or perceptions which now *have* reflexes (the other, object).

(2) A distinguishing feature of the *imperial* balance (stage two) is a self-containment that was not present before. Now the self is its enduring interests or wishes, its needs. Therefore, a self-concept can emerge. The capacity to have one's impulses, rather than be them, allows a new sense of freedom, independence, agency. The transition out of this stage of embeddedness in one's needs brings into being that need-mediating reality which we refer to when we speak of mutuality. From this perspective, it is clearer now that the evolutionary balance of stage two tilted toward independence and stage three will retain a certain freedom yet lean toward belonging. One consequence of moving the meaning of self from *being* needs (stage two) to *having* needs (stage three) is the ability to talk about feeling now *as* feelings rather than as social negotiations. For example, Kegan tells the story of a person in stage two who lied to her mother and said she felt "guilty." He discovered that what she meant by this was really a feeling of anxious anticipation of what her mother would do if her mother found out she lied. That is, the person actually felt "worried," and felt it as a social negotiation with her mother. The person could not yet feel "guilt" because guilt has to do with discomfort simply because the lie exists and one is implicated in it. Only at a more mature stage can one talk about a feeling as a feeling, not merely as a social negotiation. *During* the transition between stages this change in the construction of feeling can be felt as very perplexing. Its most common manifestation is adolescent moodiness.

Because counselors and spiritual directors deal most often with persons in stages three to five, a more thorough explanation of these stages will follow. Later, this explanation will be used to correlate issues of human maturity process with issues in Christian spirituality.

(3) In the *interpersonal* balance (stage three) the self's feelings are, by definition, shared; someone else is in there from the beginning. Its strength is its capacity to be conversational, freeing itself from the imperial balance's frenzy-creating urge to

find out what other people will do about how the self feels and acts. Its weakness lies in its inability to consult itself about that conversation, that shared reality. It cannot because the self *is* that shared reality.

At this stage, if development is imaged in first-person language, my personal conflicts are not really conflicts about what I want and what someone else wants. On closer examination, they consistently turn out to be conflicts between what I want as part of *this* shared reality and what I want as part of *that* shared reality. To ask me in this evolutionary balance to resolve such a conflict by bringing both shared realities before me is to touch precisely the limits of this way of making my self and the other. "Bringing it *before* me" means not being subject to it, being able to take it as an object, which is just what this balance cannot do.

When I live in this balance as an adult, Kegan notices, some people see me as a prime candidate for assertiveness training, for learning to stand up for myself, for allowing more "selfish" attitudes, as if these were skills to be added on to whoever else I am. Much psychological and spiritual literature will talk about me as lacking self-esteem, as being "easy" because I want other people to like me. But this does not really address me in my predicament, in what I hope for. It is not as if this self which supposedly lacks self-esteem is a self that *can* stand up for itself independently of how other people feel. It is more that there *is* no self independent of "other people liking." This self is constructed differently from one that needs confidence. The difference is not an affective matter, not a question of how much I like myself or how much self-confidence I have. The difference goes to the fundamental ground, to the way I construct the meaning of my self. This balance lacks coordination of its shared psychological space which is "pieced out" in a variety of mutualities. It lacks the self-coherence in these varieties that is the cornerstone of "identity"; in other terms, it lacks the more public coherence ordinarily meant by "ego." For Kegan, (1982, p. 96) it would be incorrect to say that an ego or identity is lacking at stage three, or that here there is a weaker ego. What there is here is a qualitatively, not a quantitatively, different ego, a different way of making the ego cohere.

Although this balance is interpersonal it is not intimate. That is because what might appear to be intimacy here is the self's *source* rather than its aim. There is no self to share with another; instead the other is necessary to bring the self into being. This is fusion, not intimacy.

This way of making the self generates action, especially in women, that can appear to be worthy of religious admiration: spending one's life caring for others, deferring to others' needs and interests. Precisely because these activities can appear to be mature Christian self-sacrifice, intimate love, or religious dedication, counselors and directors need to have a developmental perspective which prompts honest evaluation of both spiritual and personal maturity. Where women's fusion may be confused with intimacy, men's fusion may give the illusion of independence. Young men are often fused with peers whose values are "macho." That is, these young men *are* a relationship to other men who say, "Don't let any woman trap you. Women are really out to get you to marry them and lose your freedom." Some men, therefore, may appear independent but are actually fused with relationships that reinforce only male-centered, self-serving attitudes. They may use the language of independence, but the structure of their relationship is fusion. Examples of this appear at the end of this chapter and in Chapter 4.

A person in stage three is uncomfortable with anger; actually she may not even *be* angry in situations which might be expected to make a person angry. Anger owned and expressed is a risk to the interpersonal construction of the self. My getting angry, Kegan explains (p. 97), amounts to a declaration of a sense of self separate from my relation to you—that I am a person too, that I have my own feelings. It is also a declaration that you are a separate person who can survive my being angry, that it is not an ultimate matter for you. There are hundreds of reasons why people might hesitate to express anger when they feel it. But it seems that persons in this balance undergo experiences, such as being victimized by their husbands, which do not make them angry because they cannot know themselves apart from the interpersonal relationship; instead they feel sad, wounded, or incomplete. Some religious counselors interpret this lack of anger as "patience," "long-suffering," or even as "carrying the cross." As a result, they can reinforce immaturity, or even abandon a client in her *emerging* balance of a more cohesive, independent self.

(4) In differentiation from embeddedness in interpersonalism, meaning-evolution makes a self which maintains coherence in relationships and so achieves an identity. This sense of self-ownership or self-direction is its principal characteristic. In moving from "I *am* my relationships" to "I *have* relationships," there is now someone who does this having, who brings into being a kind of psychic regulation, system, or *institutional* balance (stage four).

Desire to "transcend the interpersonal" rightly meets objections from those who want to stress that other people should remain important to us throughout our lives. However, others are not lost by emergence from embeddedness in the interpersonal. On the contrary, now they are truly found. The issue is *how* other people are found. The *institutional* balance includes other people in the context of their place in the maintenance of a self-system.

A strength here is the person's new capacity for independence, the ability to own herself rather than have all the aspects of herself owned by various relationships. Feelings arising out of one's relationships no longer constitute the self; instead they are mediated by a self-system. Within this very strength lies a limit. The self is identified with the organization or system (coherence) it is trying to run smoothly. Regulation rather than mutuality is now ultimate. Here the question is not "Do you still like me?" but "Does my control still stand?" This evolutionary balance allows one that stability and integrity of personal boundaries, of deciding, in a relationship, who will get in, and when. However, the primacy of control inhibits mutuality and is still far from intimacy.

(5) The rebalancing that characterizes the fifth ego stage, *interindividual*, is, finally, the achievement of human maturity. The self is separated from identification with maintenance of the self-system or institution; there is now a self which *has* control instead of *being* control. Unlike the previous stages which tilted toward either independence or belonging, this rebalancing has both of them equally.

One's construction of human community is significant here. One now has the capacity to join others not as fellow instrumentalists (stage two), nor as partners in fusion (stage three), nor as loyalists (stage four), but as individuals who are value-originating and history-making. Whereas the institutional self brought the interpersonal "into" the self, this new construction brings the self back into the interpersonal. There now is a "self" to be brought to others, rather than derived from others. Genuine "self" sacrifice is now a possibility. Intimacy can, finally, be a reality. There is a self which can surrender its rebellious independence for freely chosen interdependence with others and with God. Now there can be fully mature Christian spirituality.

The meaning of "work" and "dedication" is revolutionized at this stage. If one no longer *is* one's self-control, neither is one any longer the duties, work roles, or career which maintaining a self-system gives rise to. Because one *has* a career rather than being a career, one is no longer vulnerable to performance-failure as an ultimate humiliation; one can "hear" negative reports about one's activities since one no longer *is* these activities. The implications for Christian ministry are obvious.

Maturity, then, is the outcome of a process of balancing the lifelong tension between the yearnings for inclusion and distinctness. Maturity is, basically, the deep personal openness which comes from having an independent identity, yet recognizing the personal limitations of independence and autonomy as the goal of development. Valuing, instead, the intimacy of mutual interdependence, the mature person is one who can freely surrender herself or himself, who can risk a genuinely mutual relationship with others and with God.

Forms and Functions of Embeddedness Cultures

Some psychologists view the "holding environment" as an idea intrinsic to infancy. Kegan (p. 116) views it as an idea intrinsic to human evolution. There is not a holding environment from which we eventually free ourselves; instead there is a life history of cultures of embeddedness. There is never an individual because the word refers only to that side of the person that is individuated or differentiated. There is always, as well, the side that is attached, is embedded. "Person" refers to the fundamental motion of evolution itself; it is as much about the side of the self that is embedded in a context (family, school, church) as that which is individuated from it. Kegan maintains that there is never just a you; and at this very moment your own flexibility or lack of it, your own sense of wholeness or lack of it, is in large part a function of how your own current embeddedness culture is holding you.

Every stage of human development, Kegan maintains (pp. 115–132), has a particular culture of embeddedness and each serves the same three functions: (1) confirmation (holding on to the person, to the me-I-am-becoming, to the experience of meaning-making); (2) contradiction (letting go of the me-I-have-been, letting go of the made-meaning as new meaning evolves); (3) remaining in place (staying put during the period of transformation so that what was me and gradually becomes not-me can be successfully reintegrated as the object of my new balance). A few examples from stages three, four, and five will clarify the way these functions can provide what Kegan calls "natural therapy."

Interpersonal Culture of Mutuality (Stage Three). The interpersonal balance is embedded in a culture of mutuality, of mutually reciprocal one-to-one relationships. This culture *confirms* the person by acknowledging and supporting the capacity for collaborative self-sacrifice in mutually attuned interpersonal relationships. Friends, family, co-workers orient the person to shared subjective experience, to "feelings," and moods. Late adolescents or young adults may spend hours talking about how they feel about people and events in their lives. This culture is helpful when it *contradicts*, when it recognizes and promotes an adult's emergence from embeddedness in interpersonalism by refusing to be fused with the person while still seeking association. That is, it is naturally therapeutic when it demands that the person assume responsibility for his own initiatives or her own preferences. It asserts the other's independence. Close examination shows that most cultures emphasize this function for men yet neglect it for women. It is important to remember that these two functions are not opposed; rather they are helpful companions. For example, when a young woman's independence is encouraged while affectionate support is also evident, she will experience the reality that autonomy is not necessarily an end to gratification. Or, in the case of a young man, he will realize that deep connection does not necessarily require the sacrifice of independence. In this stage, the third function, *continuity*, means that interpersonal partners permit the relationship to be relativized or placed in the bigger context of life's ultimate goals (e.g. religious commitment, career) and psychological self-definition (e.g. sexual identity). One's development is at high risk if one's interpersonal partners (e.g. family, friends) leave at the very time one is emerging from embeddedness.

Transition from this interpersonal stage (embeddedness in mutuality) to the institutional stage (embeddedness in personal autonomy) often occurs through the medium of going away to college, or a temporary job, or joining the military. These provide opportunities for provisional identity which both leave the interpersonal context behind and preserve it, intact, for return. It is a time-limited participation in institutional life, in a life balanced more toward independence.

Institutional Culture of Autonomy (Stage Four). The institutional balance is embedded in a culture of personal autonomy or self-authorship in love or work. Typically there is group involvement in career, some admission to the public arena. This culture *confirms* by acknowledging and supporting one's capacity for independence, self-definition, authority, exercise of personal enhancement, ambition or achievement. One is recognized as having a "career" rather than a "job," as "life partner" rather than a "helpmate." This culture supports greater maturity when it *contradicts* by recognizing and promoting an adult's emergence from embeddedness in independent self-definition. Refusal to accept mediated, non-intimate, form subordinated relationships is the most helpful form of contradiction for a person in this phase of development. *Continuity* here means that ideological forms permit themselves to be relativized on behalf of the play between forms. For example, faithful marriage partners and job security permit women and men to reconstruct the meaning of themselves as interdependent lovers and workers. Or, pastoral ministry from persons who understand religious development will be continuous and encourage adults to relinquish control for the sake of deeper relationships of interdependence. Pastoral care will be designed to encourage adults to accept vulnerability and exercise leadership so they can reintegrate their religious experience in a more mature way.

Transition from the institutional balance (embedded in personal autonomy) to the inter-individual balance (embedded in genuine intimacy, the interpenetration of self-directed persons) can come, Kegan notes, through the medium of religious or political self-surrender, or through love protected by the unavailability of the partner. At the same time one is preserving love and surrendering control of love. This transition is the heart of the story of all great saints.

Interindividual Culture of Intimacy (Stage Five). In the most mature phase of development, the one in which there is development beyond autonomy, one is embedded in a culture of intimacy. In the inter-individual balance, *confirmation* is the central function. This culture acknowledges and supports the capacity for interdependence, for self-surrender and intimacy, and for interdependent self-definition.

Cautions. All the usual cautions about making neat divisions or clear distinctions in any model of human development apply here! No person or group is entirely in one stage at one time. Because every person is a *process* of meaning making, one aspect of a person's development may be evolving into one balance of independence *and* belonging while still another dimension may be at another balance. A man's marriage relationship, for example, might be constructed in terms of an institutional self while his meaning-making in religious matters might be embedded in needs. The latter would appear in his anxiety over "what God will do if I do this." Still another caution would be to notice that many persons spend more time in transition than in any one balance of meaning-making. These cautions do not lessen the value of having a comprehensive model of development. It is to pastoral counseling and spiritual direction what a map is to a traveler. It serves as an experienced guide which promotes progress and inhibits faulty, superficial impressions, yet it cannot substitute for sustained personal experience of a place. Notice how the pastoral counselor described below can present opportunities for a client to choose growth because the counselor has an appropriate map of what greater maturity looks like.

Application to Pastoral Counseling

Lambert: Counseling the Interpersonal Self. The following is a case I have taken from Kegan (1982, pp. 184–185) and modified by making the counselor be a campus ministry chaplain who eventually invites Lambert to consider religious issues.

Lambert is a college freshman who brought himself to the campus chaplain because he was depressed and had stopped working. It was the middle of his first semester and he said he was feeling "terribly insignificant." He was living alone in a dormitory room away from home. "You could die in there," he said, "and nobody would know it until your body started to rot." He missed his parents terribly. He would call them and write to them frequently. In his communications with them he said he felt he was wasting his opportunity and their money: he was here to study and learn but he wasn't studying and he was not learning; he was letting them down.

Lambert's parents told him he owed them nothing, that they felt college was a time for all kinds of learning and that this included learning to live through difficult experiences. "What is happening to you right now," they said, "is a real part of college life, too. We are sorry that you are having a rough time, but we don't think you're wasting it; you're doing it. And you aren't letting us down."

Lambert felt tremendously betrayed and rejected by this apparently understanding and sympathetic response from his parents. "It's as though you've been a good agent of the home office all these years," the counselor suggested, "and you've met your quotas and reported in regularly." Lambert replied, "Yeah, and now I've been fired."

As Lambert continued to meet with the chaplain he was able to say that he really longed to hear his parents say to him, "Come home. Give it up and we'll take you back." He kept up the pressure on them with his complaints and sadness, but his parents would not rise to his bait and welcome him back home. Finally, when he was home for Christmas and was at close range over a longer period, his mother told him that if he wanted to quit he could, and both parents told him they would understand if his grades in the first semester were not first rate.

After returning to campus, Lambert told the chaplain he was feeling quite hurt by his parents' willingness to lower their expectations of him. He seemed to feel somehow that with their reduced expectations he was, himself, reduced. And also he felt terribly let down by what he saw as his mother's collapse through her willingness to let him come home. He started to feel that in his complaints he was not only hoping to be taken back, but that a part of him hoped they would *not* take him back, hoped they would help him by standing firm. Once he recognized this he became a lot firmer himself.

Over his next several sessions the chaplain confirmed his choice to talk about pleasing himself, about making decisions on his own that reflected his own wishes. Lambert described taking the initiative to try to date one of the most popular young women on campus, something he never would have had the courage to try in high school. She was busy, he said, but she was so nice about it that he wasn't discouraged and might call her again. The chaplain listened attentively to Lambert's conversation about his new "love life." Lambert found—paradoxically, he thought—that as he began to think more about "deciding for myself" he also began to feel less lonely. He stopped writing home and calling home so frequently, and at his last counseling session he told a story about running into a fellow student on campus who was from his old high school. The student had recently been home and had run into Lambert's father. Lambert's father had said, "If you ever see that bum of a son of mine, tell him to drop us a line; we haven't heard from him in weeks." Lambert told the story with pride and joy.

The chaplain made friendly inquiries about Lambert's religious life on campus since she had seen Lambert regularly at Sunday worship. He replied, "Everything is fine, thanks; I just wanted to talk to you about my problem with school because I figured you had seen other guys going through this same thing and you wouldn't make fun of me."

As this pastoral counselor began to develop a relationship with Lambert, her constructive developmental point of view enabled her to convey to Lambert that she understood the situation *as Lambert was experiencing it*. This enabled the counselor to *join* Lambert in his discomfort as he began to emerge from an embeddedness in the interpersonal. She saw that Lambert's grief was not so much over the loss of home as it was grief over the loss of balance, the loss of feeling at home in the world. She recognized and cultured, as Lambert's parents did, the moves toward self-authorship and psychological autonomy which characterize this new balance. The subtle and overt messages this college freshman got regarding being on his own in the conduct of his academic and social life acted to honor this longing in the newly emerging development of the self and its relationship to others.

But the chaplain realized that for a person who is only beginning this emergence, the same messages—which professors and parents may think of as confirmations of the student's adulthood—can be experienced as an abandonment, a refusal to care. Kegan images embeddedness cultures as amniotic fluid which bursts its water before passing the organism to a new evolutionary state; so the shock of college to an interpersonally embedded freshman can itself potentially provide just the experience that may lead him or her out of the current evolutionary truce. But for this to happen, the chaplain knew that there must be some context which recognized the student's discomfort and did not consider a sustained acknowledging of his grief as "hand holding." Rather it was a bridging environment that was a holding of the whole life enterprise by doing three things. First, it confirmed the capacity for relationships with family, friends, professors, and campus ministers by sharing feelings and moods. Second, it nevertheless contradicted Lambert's efforts to identify himself entirely with his comfortable way of making the meaning of himself as *being* relationships rather than *having* relationships. In other words, it recognized the old interpersonalism but refused to be swept into it. Finally, this chaplain, along with Lambert's parents, friends and teachers, fulfilled the third function of a naturally therapeutic environment when they stayed put in order to be reinterpreted and valued in a more mature way as Lambert himself grows as a person: a *process* of meaning-making.

This chaplain demonstrated a grasp of the kind of depression that is characteristic of movement out of this fusion with parents. While I will say more about depression in Chapter 6, Lambert's predicament offers an opportunity to notice several aspects of this issue now. Kegan (1982, pp. 267–273) conceives of depression as radical doubt, as not knowing the answer to such basic questions as: How do the world and I cohere? What is the meaning of my life and what is the ultimate meaning of anything? Who am I and who are these other people and who is God? The depression of each stage of life is characterized by a particular concern, and each concern can be experienced primarily as either a threat to, or a questioning of, that concern.

Lambert's depression shows concern about dependency. He feels a threat to the way he makes the meaning of himself and others, a way characterized by *being* the relationship to his parents rather than *having* the relationship. This is manifested in his feeling unbearably lonely, deserted, and betrayed. He feels others are pushing him to grow up or give up relationships with nothing to take their place. He is defending his own threatened balance of the universal longings for both inclusion and independence.

This pastoral counselor has a constructive-developmental perspective. Consequently, she understands her primary function to be support for the opportunities for meaning-evolution which Lambert brings to her as "problems." She does not seek to, and cannot, "get" Lambert to do anything; the choice is always his. She seeks only to protect the choice that presents itself in the disguise of Lambert's problems. The problems are a chance for growth, an opportunity to make the choice for the work involved in growth. The counselor holds the door open to this choice by *joining* Lambert in the experience that having such a problem entails, rather than helping to solve the problem or make the experience less painful. She chooses this approach because she is loyal to the person in his meaning-making, rather than to his stage or balance. She seeks to join the *process* of meaning evolution, rather than solve the problems which are manifestations of that process. From Lambert's point of view, this can seem like just the opposite direction from the one he wants to take. He may want to keep returning to the problem. What is the gift and grace that permits a person to move off the problem and begin the evolutionary activity of recognition? What permits a person to "hear" his or her problem rather than merely look at it?

Answering these questions in the next chapter will also reveal the reasons why Kegan's perspective is so appropriate for pastoral counseling. Applying these answers to more case studies will demonstrate some advantages of adopting Kegan's perspective for pastoral counseling.

References

Kegan, Robert. *The Evolving Self: Problem and Process in Human Development.* Cambridge, MA: Harvard University Press, 1982.

Chapter 4

Comprehensive Development: Its Significance for Pastoral Counseling

Discussion of Lambert's case, in the previous chapter, left the faith dimension only implicit. Lambert was a young man of faith who felt at ease talking to the chaplain about his loneliness; yet he declined the invitation to discuss his faith. The chaplain related to Lambert as her brother in Christ and devoted herself to supporting him in his struggle to reconstruct the meaning of himself in his dependence on his parents and his separation from them. She offered the opportunity to talk about faith and respected his negative response. Lambert, in this situation, demonstrated what Sharon Parks describes in her perceptive study, *The Critical Years: The Young Adult Search for Faith To Live By* (1986, pp. 53–60). He had a fragile inner-dependence gained from evolving out of the tension between adolescent dependence and counter-dependence. Parks shows why such inner-dependence in a young adult's psychological life would inevitably affect his life of faith. In the case of Lambert, the chaplain understood this, yet, to honor Lambert's wishes, she did not advert to faith during the counseling sessions.

In this chapter faith will become explicit in pastoral counseling. I will examine cases in which clients experience their problem as having explicitly Christian meaning. The counselor, seeking to join the person in his or her meaning-making, will therefore support the person as he or she examines the faith dimension of this meaning.

The first goal is to notice what could be gained in pastoral counseling by adopting Kegan's (1982) perspective on maturity. In order to make Kegan's perspective stand out, each case study will move in two phases. First, I will present a case as it is discussed in a standard text in pastoral counseling. Then, I will reexamine the same case using Kegan's perspective and

Christian feminist theology. Here new psychological and theological directions will emerge for the client.

The second goal concerns method for counseling. After looking at specific cases, I will point out why the characteristics of Kegan's method make it intrinsically well suited for pastoral counseling.

Cases in Pastoral Counseling of Young Adults

Case 1(a): Lambert, viewed as a guilty college student

Paul Pruyser, in "The Minister as Diagnostician" (1976), presents this case just as it was formulated and diagnosed by a pastor who is not specialized as a counselor. His vision and skills as a helper have evolved from his personal bent and standard seminary training, plus practical learning in a diversified ministry.

Description (Pruyser 1976, pp. 111–112). Lambert is a flashy-appearing, twenty year old junior at the local university. We arranged to meet in my study late one evening. In our visit that night, he stated that he was deeply upset and unable to concentrate on his studies because his girl friend had terminated their relationship.

Lambert is an active leader in his fraternity and comes from an upper-middle-class family which lives in a larger city nearby. He drives an expensive sports car and is impressed with the importance of economic security, planning to enter law school. His family has apparently some involvement in their local church, and Lambert himself has appeared in our morning worship once in a while, though he is not a registered member of the congregation. For more than a year he has been dating a popular girl who is a leader in the student government of the same university. He had not entertained thoughts of immediate marriage because of his plans for going to law school. Lambert felt torn now, he said, between a dedication to study in order to achieve the good grades needed for his long-range plans and the necessity for devoting time and energy to dealing with the crisis in his relationship with the girl.

He said he felt crushed and rejected by her action. He is anguished over the girl's decision to date an older student to whom she had taken a liking in preference to him, although Lambert himself, on becoming aware of this, had insisted on her making a choice. He had telephoned her constantly during the past two weeks, even interrupting her three times during an important sorority meeting, in an effort to win her back or to force her into making a decision about him. Now that she has chosen to date the older student, Lambert is mystified about what she can see in that other man. He suspects her to be sexually involved with the other student, for he knows, he said, that she is spending considerable time in his apartment.

Lambert described his own sexual involvement with the girl for nearly a year. His intercourse with her had been based on his deep love for her. He had taken strong initiative in the beginning, and her cooperation had only come later. He now feels that if the sexual intimacy did not stem from mutual love that would have led to marriage, it must have been based on an illusion and would not have been the "good thing" to do. He recalled an incident when he had come back to see his girl late one summer evening. They had fallen passionately into each other's arms the moment they met, had driven out in his car to a secluded place, and had intercourse. With considerable emotion he described how, afterward, she had sobbed uncontrollably for a long time. He had felt "dirty" about the sexual relationship; he had deceived himself and "offended God." He had gone out into the field by himself and prayed desperately about the matter for an hour, without coming to any peace about it.

Diagnosis (Pruyser, pp. 113–115). Lambert's coming to see me, though he had only a nominal acquaintance with me, suggested that he felt the need to get a religious or pastoral perspective on his problem. My intuition was confirmed by the emotional intensity with which he alluded to a sense of sin about the exploitive character of his sexual relationship. I tried to help Lambert clarify his feelings and thoughts, starting by discussing the impact of the girl's rejection on his feelings of self-worth. We explored the possibility that though premarital sexual intercourse was the "in" thing on campus, he himself seemed to feel deep down that it was not the right thing for him to do. He felt guilty over having pressed the girl into sexual intimacy, and suspected that his sexual aggressiveness had undermined the love and respect which had been part of their previous relationship. Could the girl have felt that she was treated as a sex object only, and not as a precious human being who is a child of God? Lambert increasingly expressed his regret over this aspect of his behavior; later in the conversation he came close to confessing the sinfulness of it, seemingly groping for a theological interpretation of his attitudes. He did, however, come through with a clear sense of repentance and regret, not only over his past action but with a movement toward deciding to act differently in the future.

In view of Lambert's nascent sense of sin and repentance, it seemed less appropriate to remind him explicitly of God's forgiving grace than to assure him of God's loving providential care for the whole of his life. He picked this up by dwelling on the positive elements of his friendship with the girl, as if to contrast his feeling of uncleanliness with feelings of gratitude. I reminded him that the path to a new harmony with God and to a new sense of cleanness and respect for himself consisted not merely in regretting the past, but, more importantly, in resolving not to let his sexual aggressiveness undermine future relationships. This part of the discussion had a calming effect on Lambert, suggesting that clarity about his wrongdoing was less threatening than leaving his thoughts and feelings in a diffuse, bewildering state.

Though Lambert spoke of a personal faith, to which his praying in the field testified, it was essentially a very privatistic dimension of his life. If his faith had been shared in greater communion with others, he might have been helped to envisage more fully the social implications of that faith. As it was, Lambert seemed to find his primary sense of communion in secular form, with his fraternity brothers. But in seeking pastoral help, he also acted on some longing to restore a bond with other believers, perhaps even to place himself under their spiritual guardianship in order to maintain his basic values.

His current crisis highlighted a profound disjunction in his values, however. Though he had some sense of awe and respect for a God to whom he could turn in personal prayer, and whom he could approach through a pastor, he had considerable awe of himself. His view of life was strongly self-centered, and in his relations to others he seemed bent on seeking mostly his own satisfaction.

I prayed with him, recognizing our human need to love and be loved, our powerful sexual passions, our temptations to self-ishness, our ability to learn from mistakes, and God's forgive-ness and help in relating ourselves to other persons in humane ways. I think that Lambert's search for pastoral light on his problem gave him some degree of liberation from bondage to his selfishness and helped set him on the way toward a more promising future, with greater sensitivity to others as well as himself. But he still has a considerable wilderness to travel.

Case 1 (b): Lambert viewed as emerging from an interper-sonal balance into a fragile institutional balance: young adult faith

What does Kegan's constructive-developmental model of maturity contribute to a counselor's ability to offer pastoral ministry to Lambert? A new diagnosis, based on Kegan's theory of personality and method for counseling, will answer this question.

Description. I will use the previous description of Lambert, a junior in college who is upset over the breakup with his girl-friend. Two changes will be made in the counseling situation. The counselor will become the chaplain introduced in Chapter 3 as counseling "Lambert." Lambert will become the same young man who, as a freshman, approached this chaplain two years earlier to talk about his relationship to his parents. These changes influence the diagnosis.

Diagnosis: new response using Kegan's model of maturity. I welcomed Lambert as a friend and brother in Christ whom I began to know two years earlier when he talked to me about his depression and loneliness as a freshman. Then, as now, my goal is twofold. First, I want to be his companion, to join him *in the experience* that having his problem entailed. This means being a guest in "his space," listening to him in order to grasp his experience and convey to him, in language he accepts as correct, the meaning he is now making of himself and others. Second, I want to offer opportunities for him to choose to do the work of evolving into greater maturity—that is, into more authentic self-direction and into deeper relationships.

Having talked to Lambert before, I realize that he is only beginning to make the meaning of himself as *having* relationships rather than *being* relationships. His current problem reflects this same process of making meaning. He is "torn between" dedication to study in order to get into law school and the necessity of devoting time to dealing with the crisis in his relationship with his girlfriend. We talked a while so that I could listen carefully to Lambert's communication of his experience as he experiences it.

Gradually, I discern that diagnosing Lambert as selfish and sexually aggressive does not address him in his predicament. Rather, he feels the threat of loss of a most important relationship (to his girlfriend), a loss that feels like the loss of himself because, at this point, he is the relationship. He feels "rejected," "crushed." He fears abandonment. I tried to understand the meaning of the fact that Lambert himself had terminated the relationship. He had insisted that his friend choose immediately between him and the older student she dated. She chose the older person and Lambert chose not to see her again. Grasping his experience of the termination enabled me to join him more fully in his process of growth.

Lambert was experiencing the pain of the conflict of creating the meaning of himself as part of two equally valued relationships. He *is* a relationship to his fraternity brothers who reinforce expectations of a career in law with the money and status and independence that go with it. Many of them see marriage as a "trap," speak of sexual relationships as "scoring," and mock and belittle men who do not speak about women the same way. Also, Lambert *is* a relationship to the young woman he loves. Her expectations include career *and* marriage. She believes that graduate school and marriage are compatible. She says that "love is the most important thing." Lambert is, therefore, part of this relationship and part of the other relationship. He feels "torn apart," he says, because he wants both but is convinced that his career possibilities will suffer if he is too "involved" in a relationship with his girlfriend.

I realize that Lambert is beginning to see the problem of fusing with relationships as the ultimate way of making the meaning of himself and others. He feels the threat to the very meaning of himself involved in relativizing what he has made the ultimate. The conflict is so strong between Lambert's expectations as a fraternity brother/pre-law student and his expectations as his girlfriend's lover that he can only relieve the tension by forcing his girlfriend to choose either an exclusive relationship to him, which Lambert believes he must subordinate to his career plans, or terminate the relationship. Lambert does not yet have an "I" to whom he can bring these conflicting feelings and values. Understanding this enables me to grasp how I can best join Lambert as he makes the meaning of himself and others in his world which feels so unstable as to be threatening.

First, I can be his companion by realizing that I, too, am a hanger-in-the-balance of the yearnings for belonging and for independence. Recalling my own struggles to be self-directed without losing relationships, I am attentive to Lambert as he communicates his present experience of these same longings. His experience is different from mine, but his longings sound very familiar.

Second, I can join Lambert in a way that offers a chance for him to choose the work of growth toward greater maturity. This means that I must be a guest in Lambert's home, listening in order to convey to him that I grasp the experience of his problem *as he experiences it.* I must be cautious that I do not move Lambert to my "turf" of psychological interpretation. Eventually, Lambert agrees that I "have it right." "Yeah," he says, "I feel pulled apart." "It's as though I am afraid that if I disagree with the guys they won't even care enough about me to talk about it or fight about it; they might just laugh and then avoid me; they might just start to leave me out of things. I'll be a nobody on campus. Then when I'm with Sharon (his girlfriend) I want to be so close to her, but I don't know what to do when she sobs uncontrollably. I don't know what's the matter with

her. I don't know how to act, and I can't stand that feeling."
Another time he says, "I feel that I have offended God by getting into a sexual relationship with Sharon. Everything has gone
wrong for us, now, and I think that it must be partly due to the
fact that it was not what God wanted for us."

Third, I want to be alert so that I do not become a co-conspirator to the balance (of relationship and differentiation) that
Lambert is defending. I want to join him in the meaning he is
beginning to make of himself and others, not the meaning he
has made so comfortably before but which now is changing and,
therefore, feels threatening. I want to companion his experience not by giving assurance or by resolving his problem, not
by getting him to do something such as be reconciled with
Sharon, for to do any of this would be to *abandon* Lambert the
person who is now beginning to "hear" the problem of locating
the meaning of himself *as* relationship. My greatest gift to Lambert is to resist speaking from outside his current frame of reference so that he will not be able to locate the meaning of himself as a relationship to me, the chaplain. My gift to refuse to
give "my opinion" about what he should do or feel, to resist
being the "other" Lambert needs in order to survive. This is
especially important in this situation because Lambert's guilty
feelings involve some "other"—God, in this case—whose
expectations are not met. Lambert feels he has offended God,
but he does not speak about this as a matter of his own standard
of conduct.

The initial effect of this way of joining Lambert's life was
an experience of loss. He lost the person which his defended
balance was hoping to hold, by whom he hoped to hold that
balance together. He was willing to continue talking with me,
nevertheless, partly because he was intrigued by the fact that
I, as a chaplain and a woman, was remaining with his yearning
to be chosen by Sharon, and to be accepted by his fraternity
brothers, and was concentrating on those issues rather than on
condemning him for sexual sins or elaborately assuring him of
God's forgiveness. On the other hand, I was not "mothering"
him; that is, I was not excusing him or feeling sorry for him but,
rather, peacefully remaining with him as a friend and compan-

ion who could be there to support [the old] Lambert while the emerging [uncomfortable] Lambert could say what he "really feels" about career, women, sex, marriage, law school, God, moral rules, the church. Some of Lambert's ideas and feelings were very negative about everything "the church" or "women" want. Many times he was simply "against" everything without being able to say much about what he was "for." After three or four conversations, Lambert began to trust that I was understanding his experience *as he experienced it* and I was willing to talk with him as one adult to another, and would not "give my opinion" about whether what he did was right or wrong. Although Lambert grew more vocal about his own opinions he did not lessen his interest in "what God wants" regarding morality. Lambert was wondering how he could be both an adult and an "obedient child of God," as he had been taught.

This led into the topic of the prodigal son and conversations which became the heart of the pastoral counseling sessions. Lambert's developmental process called for an image of God which could support the emerging self-direction that was becoming Lambert's way of making the meaning of himself and others. His previous faith had given him an image of God as parent and himself as child, an image that contradicted his current understanding of himself. Therefore, he found himself losing faith in this God in order to be "true to himself." Again, he felt "torn apart"; indeed, his faith development was moving in rhythm with his psychological life. Healing of Lambert's torn faith came through our conversation about and prayer with Luke 15:11–32, following the interpretation suggested by Sandra Schneiders' feminist theology (1986, pp. 46–47).

Schneiders shows how Jesus presents the fatherhood of God as the very antithesis of patriarchy in which there is only one adult in any family and women and children may never be self-directed. Lambert and I examined the parable together noticing how the older son embodies the patriarchal understanding of social relations. He boasts that he has been a perfect son, serving loyally and never transgressing a single command, whereas his younger brother, by assuming autonomy and making his own (foolish) choices about his inheritance, has rebelled against the very principle of patriarchy according to which children may never become true adults. But to the older son's fury, the father aligns himself with the younger son. It was the father, after all, who had not only permitted but even enabled the boy's rebellion. We noticed that it is the father who renounces the patriarchal right to punish the rebel and welcomes him home with prodigal celebration. Not only does the father decline the older son's challenge to vindicate the patriarchal principle, he even brushes aside the younger son's confused willingness to re-enter the patriarchal structure by assuming the role of a servant. On the contrary, we discussed at length how the father receives the young man as the son he has never ceased to be, and how this parable reveals that God's forgiving love, not human evil, determines God's relationship to us. What Lambert found so healing and affirming was the image of the father, far from asserting patriarchal superiority and privilege, recognizing the younger son as his equal, that is, as an adult. To the father, the son's return to the household, like his leaving, is an act of adult freedom. The relationship between them is not one of offended domination to rebellious submission but one of freely offered love asking and accepting love in return. This, Lambert came to recognize, was the answer to his own heart's question regarding faith *and* relationships to his fraternity brothers and to Sharon: Can I claim "my own ground" and still be in relationship? The answer from this word of God is a resounding yes. Even the biblical form of the answer affirms our freedom because it is given in a parable which is the most non-coercive form of teaching. It invites our attention and involvement and interpretation; it does not proclaim conclusions. Like God, a parable waits patiently until we freely "get the point" of new life: freely chosen love.

With God, I, too, patiently companioned Lambert as he chose to do the growth work which eventually bore fruit in his more mature life of faith and human relationships. My own life of faith also grew. There is a sense in which I did not know fully what the parable of the prodigal son meant until it "dawned" on me in the counseling situation. I, too, had to choose to grow by allowing Lambert and this text to "intrude" upon me, to teach me anew how authentic union with God increases rather than diminishes our human freedom, how God empowers us beyond what we can ask or imagine (Eph 3:20).

Method. This pastoral counseling method provided a naturally therapeutic environment, or culture of embeddedness, in which Lambert could choose to do the work of growth associated with the evolution natural to his emerging way of making the meaning of himself and others. It fulfilled the three functions of a healthy culture of embeddedness. First, I *confirmed* his yearning to be chosen, to be accepted, to belong to his fraternity and to belong in a loving relationship with Sharon. Second, I *contradicted* his desire to "fuse" with his fraternity brothers and with Sharon, as two years ago I had contradicted his fusion with his parents while he was a lonely freshman. Through my refusal to "give my opinion" about his actions, while at the same time conveying my deep interest in his feelings and opinions, I insisted that Lambert assume responsibility for his own initiatives and preferences. Lambert eventually called Sharon and began to demonstrate to himself and to her that they could place their relationship in the bigger context of their college life and find a way to love each other that allowed them to be "really close" without submerging themselves into each other's wishes and values. Third, I became part of Lambert's wider culture of embeddedness that was *staying around* in order to be reintegrated into an even more mature balance of belonging and independence. His parents' continued their earlier healthy parenting by supporting Lambert's independence while demonstrating his secure place in their lives. His friend Sharon remained willing to be Lambert's friend. But now they were learning together how to find an appropriate balance of adult independence and adult interdependence. His fraternity brothers, too, remained associated with Lambert, but they had the most difficulty in allowing Lambert to relativize his relationship to them. They tended, rather, to confirm Lambert in a male-centered exaggeration of independence and made it difficult for Lambert to share any aspect of his life in which he might feel awkward or vulnerable. I remained Lambert's friend to whom he could relate as adult to adult.

My pastoral counseling method was also a culture in which Lambert's faith could develop. His faith also needed confirmation, contradiction, and continuity. I *confirmed* his desire to seek God's will for him—that is, to grasp God's attitude toward him, how "God feels about me." The parable of the prodigal son revealed God's love, patient care, and affirmation of Lambert's freedom. Love and care were divine qualities Lambert had heard about many times before; "affirming my freedom," he said, "was certainly a revelation to me!" Second, I *contradicted* his unexamined acceptance of an image of God as one who demanded that Lambert fuse with God and be controlled by God. This contradiction was essential; for unless Lambert could find a new image of God he would either lose his faith or become a deeply divided person who compulsively conformed to the faith of his childhood in one compartment of his life, and defended the rest of his life from contact with this religious faith which was incompatible with adulthood. Meditation on this parable and heartfelt prayer responding to this attitude of God toward him was central to pastoral counseling with Lambert. Third, I *continued* after the formal counseling sessions to relate to Lambert as a mentor. Sharon Parks (1986, p. 86) explains the significance of this relationship for a young adult as one of "inviting into greater strength." It is important to note that those who serve the mentoring function can be distinguished from the heroes and heroines of adolescent devotion. The mentor holds a very significant degree of power, but the fusion quality is absent. Mentors anchor the vision of the potential self. They beckon the self into being and exercise intellectual and emotional appeal and support. But the young adult exercises at least a rudimentary sense of critical choice. He or she accepts the older adult as mentor only when the mentor's advice corresponds with his or her own experience. Indeed, the young adult will even make do without a mentor rather than betray the integrity of the emerging self. Lambert accepted me as a mentor for his emerging adult faith. He also began associating with students he met at discussions and worship services sponsored by our campus ministry team. Campus ministry's theme, "developing adult faith," became Lambert's personal quest.

Case 2(a): Elizabeth, viewed as an acutely uncomfortable "adulteress" referred by her psychiatrist
This case also is presented in Pruyser, *The Minister As Diagnostician* (1976).

Description (Pruyser, pp. 115–116). Although I have known Elizabeth for some time as a visitor to my church, the pastoral contact she sought with me came at the behest of her psychiatrist. She is a woman in her mid-twenties with attractive appearance, from a rural church background and with a college education. Earlier, when she was working to help her husband get through graduate school, their preschool daughter was enrolled in the church's day care center, a contact which also brought the family occasionally to worship.

Elizabeth phoned me at the church one morning, asking for an appointment to visit about "an important personal problem." When we met the next day, she explained that a divorce, initiated some time ago by her husband, had become final, and that she was now seeing a psychiatrist in order to help her through the process of adjustment. She is pursuing additional college study in order to qualify for work to support herself and her daughter, of whom she has custody. Currently, she finds it difficult to concentrate on her studies, to fall asleep at night, and to make plans for her future. She feels burdened with an overwhelming sense of guilt, which has paralyzing effects on her whole life. No matter how hard she has tried, she cannot free herself from the power of these guilt feelings, and her psychiatrist had suggested that she discuss this aspect of her situation with a minister. I felt all the more encouraged by this referral to engage Elizabeth in pastoral conversation with a definite religious focus.

Elizabeth made no secret of the fact that she held herself blameworthy for the divorce. When her parents attempted to blame her ex-husband for it, she had told them the truth, namely, that she had had an affair with another man, which was the real cause of the marriage failure. Though she and her ex-husband had enjoyed a fairly good marriage, his preoccupation with his studies had left her very lonely and vulnerable to the attentions of a married man with whom she worked. She felt that this affair was morally wrong and that it had brought about the painful consequences she now suffered. She felt she had "sinned against God," deserved to be punished, and needed forgiveness, but doubted that it could be granted.

Diagnosis (Pruyser, pp. 116–118). I sensed that Elizabeth had ample awareness of God's holiness and that this intensified her feelings of guilt over her wrongdoing. Her sense of guilt was vivid and powerful, giving her no respite. She assumed the whole responsibility for the marriage failure, in no way sparing herself, even to the point of discounting her ex-husband's part in letting things go as far as they went. She was indeed repentant enough, in fact punishing herself through her sleeplessness and her inner turmoil. So I helped her explore the dimensions of responsibility, her ex-husband's share of it, and the nature of her feelings of sinfulness.

Sensing her inability to accept God's forgiving grace, I felt that the words of a pastor as "man of God" were needed to move her beyond a confession of sin to restoration in grace. I reminded her that faith in God consists not only in doing what is right, but in accepting his personal love of us, no matter what our moral failures are. We remembered that God's sending his Son is the clear sign of his unbreakable love for each person. I retold for her the story of the woman caught in adultery (Jn 8:3–11), whom Jesus had not condemned, but set free with the admonition not to sin again. I applied the meaning of this story to her life, saying that although God did not approve her wrongdoing, his final will was for her not to stand condemned but to regain life. I affirmed her in her struggle to find a new life, noting that, if punishment was needed, she had punished herself quite enough already. In view of her sincere regret I assured her that God offered her his gift of total forgiveness in order that she could be free from the power of her sin and guilt feelings, moving into the full life for which she was destined in Christ.

In response to this story, Elizabeth identified herself with the woman caught in adultery, breaking into tears at the assurance of God's will for freedom for her. When she heard pastoral words of forgiveness in terms directly related to the content of her religious faith, coming from a religious authority, she felt relieved and grateful.

It was plain that Elizabeth trusted me, as she had earlier trusted the church's day care center for her daughter. Yet it had been difficult for her to experience a sense of God's providence, his loving care and guidance, in the midst of these painful events in her life. I suspect that her relatively distant relation to a community of faith and love left her inadequate opportunity for experiencing providence through other persons sharing her faith and calling her attention to "the other side of God."

A prayer shared with Elizabeth lifted to God her feeling of overwhelming guilt, thanking him for his power to destroy those oppressive feelings, and to set her free from them. I prayed that she would be filled with a new sense of well-being and the loving and forgiving presence of God in her life. Elizabeth said that she felt greatly relieved and that she deeply appreciated our visit.

Case 2(b): Elizabeth, viewed as invested in the interpersonal and struggling for young adult faith

Revised Description. I will begin with the description of Elizabeth given in the previous case (2a) and change the pastoral counselor into the same university chaplain described in Case 1(b), the counselor informed by Kegan's model of maturity. Elizabeth met this chaplain when Elizabeth's husband was in graduate school and they lived close to the campus and went to the campus worship services and enrolled their daughter in the university's child-development center. Elizabeth felt at ease speaking to a woman engaged in pastoral ministry.

New Diagnosis, using Kegan's model of maturity and Christian feminist theology. I welcome Elizabeth as my sister in Christ and listen attentively to her description of her experience. I want to reflect back to her that I grasp it *the way she experienced it.* Elizabeth soon realizes that I need her "corrections" and "modifications" in order to know that I grasp her experience "correctly."

Elizabeth's life and therefore her life of faith are largely invested in the interpersonal balance. Unlike a male of her age whose male culture exaggerates the value of independence and undervalues relationships, Elizabeth's female culture has taught her that every feeling must be mediated through the interpersonal. A "good woman" lives for others; indeed, paying attention to one's own needs can only be selfish and against the will of God. Elizabeth and a man of similar age (e.g. Lambert) could be *the same* in the *way* they both make the meaning of themselves: they *are* relationships rather than *have* relationships. They are *very different*, nevertheless, regarding *what* those relationships tell them is their meaning. Lambert, for example, is a self who is part of several relationships that give conflicting messages. His fraternity brothers say, "Don't get trapped into commitments to a woman." His girlfriend says, "Let's plan a life together." Therefore, he feels "torn apart." Elizabeth's self, on the other hand, is fused with different relationships that all say the same thing: serving others is good and holy, autonomy is selfish and bad. Elizabeth, however, acted to satisfy her own need for affection and for mutual sharing by having an affair when her husband was preoccupied with study and expected her to be his complete housekeeping and childcare system. She therefore feels "guilty." She has taken initiative and acted independently. This is what really seems strange or "wrong" to her. Elizabeth's God also tells her that disobedience, that is, independence, is sinful. Consequently, her sense of guilt is twofold, strong, and unrelenting.

Knowing these two sources of guilt enables me to know how to join Elizabeth, as a counselor, in the evolution of the meaning of her self and her faith. First, I remain with her in her yearning to be accepted, to be loved, to belong, to give herself to her daughter, to be a woman of faith. I convey to her that I grasp her experience as she experiences it: she feels that it must be her fault, her sin that she could not just suffer and patiently endure the "hurt" she felt at not being able to elicit her husband's attention to her need for affection and conversation or not being able to get his cooperation in caring for their daughter. She feels that she had no right to respond to affection from another man. She admits that she also felt like "getting back" at her husband by "showing him" that someone else thought she was desirable and smart even if her husband did not.

As Elizabeth gradually feels that I am her companion in the way she makes the meaning of herself and others, she begins to feel also that this self might "hold together" against the threat. The threat is in the form of a radical doubt about who she is. In other words, she begins to get the sense that she will be safe even if she "looks" away from the threat raised by her independent attitude and begins to attend elsewhere, namely to her own preferences and her own needs. This can happen because I not only *confirm* her yearnings but also do a second thing. I allow her [old] self to fall away in safety and allow her to do her own work of growth by *resisting* being an "other" she needs in order to survive. I resist speaking from outside her frame of reference so that she will not locate her self as a relationship to this other.

As Elizabeth begins to speak about her own needs and preferences, we review the familiar gospel story of the woman discovered in adultery. Elizabeth joins me in examining more of Jesus' teaching about marriage and adultery. Elizabeth herself begins to make connections between Jesus' teaching and her own situation. She begins to notice that Jesus did not condemn the adulterous woman and then forgive her. He did not condemn her at all (Jn 8:11), so neither does he condemn Elizabeth. She sees that the men who brought the adulteress to Jesus are shown as "not without sin." What is more, the focus of Jesus' teaching about adultery is men's equal responsibility in marital infidelity; that is, Jesus was *contradicting* the assumption that adultery "was all the woman's fault." Elizabeth permitted herself to "hear the word of God and keep it" in her heart. She opened herself to this healing acceptance of Jesus. She heard, also, the way Jesus affirmed the Syro-Phoenecian woman's audacity (Mk 7:24–30), and how Jesus presented himself as God's Wisdom (Mt 11:28–30) who, in the Hebrew bible, is imaged as a woman.

Elizabeth began to correlate these teachings with her own experience. She began to "hear" the *experience* that having her problem entailed. She gradually heard herself feeling not so much "hurt" that she could not elicit her husband's attention to her needs, but actually angry, and frustrated that he refused to do his share of parenting and controlled their relationship and subordinated everything to his plans for study and work. She heard her real "sin" more as avoidance and passivity than lust or pride. She realized that she always avoided conflict assuming it was "uncharitable" and, thus, detrimental to relationships. We examined the consequences of this assumption and she had insight into Jean Baker Miller's theme (1976): conflict inevitably goes with the negotiation necessary for authentic mutuality and sharing. Elizabeth noticed a pattern of passive aggressive behavior toward her husband. She was unable to say directly to her husband, "Your actions make me feel isolated and angry." Instead, she ceased cooperating with her husband's style of marriage, and responded to the affection demonstrated by another man.

Most of all, Elizabeth heard Jesus' word calling her to be converted from a sinful pattern of avoidance and passivity to a saintly pattern of free, inner-directed love for herself, her daughter, her former husband, and everyone she worked with. She felt called also to continue growing in awareness of God's maternal support and affirmation of her, qualities of God that she could recognize in her own maternal desire for her daughter's maturity.

Besides confirming and contradicting aspects of the way Elizabeth made the meaning of herself, I offered the gift of continuity. I stayed around to be her friend and mentor in the ways of adult faith.

Method in Pastoral Counseling

Need to Articulate Theological and Psychological Criteria

For the past twenty-five years eclecticism has gained adherents in pastoral counseling. Research on the outcome of therapies has made it increasingly difficult to argue that one therapeutic orientation is predictably more successful than others. Practitioners acknowledge their eclectic orientation, regardless of the theory in which they were trained. A growing emphasis on the theological foundations of pastoral counseling also reveals variety and combinations.

As this trend continues pastoral counselors might well heed Clyde J. Steckel's advice in *Clinical Handbook of Pastoral Counseling* (1985, p. 28). Articulate your theological understanding of pastoral counseling, he recommends, so that one avoids the aimless pursuit of fads and so that the criteria of pastoral objectives and methods becomes theologically articulated. Otherwise social norms for a healthy personality can dominate pastoral practice, or the incompatibility between one's theology and one's theory of personality can go undetected.

The theological criteria for the counseling objectives and methods I used in the cases of Lambert and Elizabeth (and for cases that will appear in the next section of the book) are based on two theological sources: scripture and Christian spiritual tradition.

Biblical theology is not used in the sense of merely moral rules given in scripture. Clients' problems are not measured in terms of prohibitions against adultery, divorce, or fornication. These biblical teachings are surely accepted and examined in the light of contemporary interpretations, such as Philip Keane's *Sexual Morality: A Catholic Perspective* (1977). The focus, however, is on the biblical pattern of God's interaction with us.

Three biblical patterns form the standard for appropriate pastoral counseling. First, God waits, and loves, and does not coerce us. Jesus' parables of the prodigal son and of the wheat and chaff, for example, reinforce the experience of Israel's history in which God invites, supports, and tries to elicit a free response of love. Second, God heals and calls us through human love and the care of the community. Third, God's call and commandment is always to love, freely given; indeed, relationships and adult responsibility for one's faith are central. In other words, the longing for freedom and for belonging are equally affirmed in scripture.

Principles of Christian spiritual tradition also influence the objectives and methods demonstrated in the case studies. That is, they follow the patterns of the experience of holy persons tested over a lifetime of growth and development. A primary principle is: grace works through the processes of history and nature. This is a central theme of Karl Rahner's (1978) theology of God's self-communication in and through our ordinary life (pp. 126–133). Another principle is: union with God through grace does not relieve us of the effort to discern or judge the appropriate response to God's presence in the events of our life. Discernment, as Ernest Larkin (1981) explains, requires self-directed judgments based on critical self-knowledge and the ability to trust and evaluate our experience of God; otherwise it is compulsion, conformity to external authority, or reading tea leaves. This principle, then, gives equal honor to relationship (to God, others, and oneself) and to self-direction or autonomy. The third principle is: self-knowledge is essential to every stage of the spiritual life. For example, Teresa of Avila teaches in *The Interior Castle* (1980, p. 291) that no matter how advanced one is in the mansions of prayer, one can never neglect self-knowledge.

The psychological criteria follow Robert Kegan's constructive-developmental theory of personality because it contributes to pastoral counseling some effective tools for interpreting the logic of human action. That is, human actions are seen to follow the logic of the evolution of meaning-making as described in Kegan's five stages of development.

Kegan's Psychological Method Fits These Theological Criteria

Counseling with Lambert and Elizabeth has demonstrated a method that follows the theological criteria explained above. It enables the counselor and client to enter into the very process revealed by Jesus as God's own way of liberating and healing us. That is, it enables us to participate in the mystery of God's redemptive love according to the biblical patterns and principles of Christian spirituality given in the previous section.

First, the focus of pastoral counseling is meaning-making. As the ministry of Jesus is to reveal the meaning of life as the opportunity to enter freely into a loving relationship with God as adult daughters and sons, so the ministry of counseling concentrates on the person *as a process of making meaning.* This process is understood as one which involves these two longings which were addressed by Jesus: desire for free self-direction and for close relationship. Kegan's model includes both longings at every stage of human development.

Second, the pastoral counselor's goal is to *join* the person in her or his evolution of meaning. A person's presenting problem always reflects a process of making the meaning of herself or himself in relationship to others. The counselor resonates to the *experience* that having such a problem entails. This is the constructive-developmental version of psychodynamic "transference." For example, Lambert's presenting problem, in his freshman year, was depression and loneliness. The counselor joined Lambert's *experience* of the feeling of fusion with his parents, the sense of having the boundaries of this fused self threatened by being away at college. In his junior year, Lambert's presenting problem is the inability to study. This problem is a symptom or manifestation of his *experience* of being "torn." The counselor joined Lambert in his experience of the "pulling apart" that results from his making the meaning of himself through fusion with two basic relationships (with fraternity brothers and girlfriend) which promote contrasting longings: for both independence and connection. The tension is not in the longings so much as in the way Lambert makes the meaning of self.

"Joining persons in their experience" is also a way of describing the mystery of divine Incarnation. For example, the fourth gospel prologue hymns the Incarnation as the act of God's word becoming human flesh, becoming one with us. And Philippians 2:6–8 reminds us that Christ emptied himself and took on full humanity. Is that not another way of saying that the redemptive process was one of joining persons in their experience, in their evolution of the meaning of themselves, others, and God?

Third, this method of pastoral counseling is effective because it is client-centered in a special way. Insofar as it is mutual and egalitarian it is authentically Christian. As Jesus calls us friends, not servants, so the counselor joins the client as a companion, as one who also "hangs in the balance" of connection and autonomy, as one who journeys with, not above, persons as part of their evolution of meaning. This controlling image of maturity allows the counselor to see herself as involved in the same life process of balancing independence and attachment as the client; instead of seeing herself as the "healthy" one who helps the "sick" person, she sees herself as also striving to make the meaning of herself and others by balancing the tension between distinctness and inclusion. As Jesus was a guest in the home of Zacchaeus and of Martha and Mary, so, too, the counselor is a guest in the client's life, listening in order to reflect back her own experience in language *she* accepts as correct. As Jesus' patient and loving presence, in the Spirit, empowers his disciples to choose the work of growth in love and responsibility, so, too, it is the counselor's supportive presence to the person understood as *a process of making meaning* that enables the person to choose to grow.

How can a person move off of seeing a problem and begin the evolutionary activity of "hearing" her problem? It is always mysterious, Kegan reminds us (1982, p. 274), even when we have some idea of how to move. Elizabeth, for example, enters counseling because she feels threatened. She can move and grow if she can get a sense that her self will hold together against this threat even if she attends elsewhere. How can she get this sense? She gets it from a counselor who is client-centered as a companion to her experience; from a counselor who has a theory of personality that is sufficiently attuned to longings for both relationship and autonomy and how they function in her way of making meaning; from a counselor who gives unconditional acceptance not simply to the meaning she has made of herself, but, rather to her as a *process* of meaning-making that always values both connection and autonomy; from a counselor who does not move her to the counselor's territory of interpretation but moves into her experience in order to convey to her that she understands her experience as she, herself, experiences it; from a counselor who holds her as an *emerging* balance of autonomy and connection, and is not a co-conspirator to her defensive balance; from a counselor who knows and feels what to confirm and what to contradict, according to Elizabeth's developmental stage.

Confirmation and resistance are different for persons in different emerging balances of connection and autonomy. Allowing seduction and manipulation of the counselor is *always abandonment* of the client in her or his emerging balance. With a client who is emerging from embeddedness in the interpersonal, that is, from making the meaning of herself as being relationships rather than having relationships, the counselor will remain with her yearning to be chosen while resisting being the "other" she needs in order to survive. The counselor will convey to the client that she grasps the client's desire to be accepted by friends while contradicting the client's insistence that she give "her opinion" about what to do. With another client who is emerging from embeddeness in autonomy and control of himself as a system of work and love relationships, the counselor will remain attentive to the client's yearning for dignity while resisting the temptation to be a "consultant" to the client's administration of his life. The counselor will convey her grasp of the client's desire for self-respect while refusing to be manipulated into acting as a "fellow believer" in the distorted beliefs through which the client's relationships are mediated. Instead, the counselor will cooperate only with the emerging balance toward intimacy. That is, the counselor will hold firmly to the value of vulnerability and the conviction that feelings of weakness are inevitable, not shameful, when one has authentic intimacy and genuinely human work relationships.

Fourth, this mode of pastoral counseling is theologically well founded because it envisions maturity beyond autonomy. Like the biblical call to surrender to love and dedicate oneself to work that is a form of bearing one another's burdens, this vision of counseling supports a person's emerging into free, adult surrender (self-directed relationship) and surrendering adulthood (reliquishing control as the ultimate value and allowing the vulnerability that mutuality and intimacy require). It takes full account of the two yearnings which are central to all narratives of religious and human experience: desire to be included and to be independent. What is more, this approach recognizes the equal dignity of each yearning. Consequently, it is a corrective to all present developmental frameworks that are biased toward autonomy. The latter consistently define growth in terms of differentiation and increasing autonomy, and lose sight of the theological truth that maturity is equally about union with God and the free, adult surrender that makes that union authentically human. Theories of development that are biased toward autonomy also lose sight of the fact that adaptation is equally about integration and attachment. As earlier chapters of this book point out, the result of this bias has been that differentiation (the stereotypically male overemphasis) is favored with the language of growth and development, while attachment (the stereotypically female over-emphasis) gets referred to in terms of dependency and immaturity. The method of pastoral counseling used here, following Kegan, is less easily bent to this prejudice because it listens equally to women's and men's expressions of their own experience and values both longings of the human heart at every stage of development. It is far different from Jung's theory of the complementarity of symbolically "masculine" and "feminine" characteristics in each person. For Jung's notion of "the feminine," as Demaris Wehr (1987) explains, is extrapolated entirely from the theory of male ego development without ever testing its explanation of "the feminine" against women's own understanding of themselves. In contrast, Kegan listens, from the beginning, equally to women and men. He can, therefore, legitimately generalize (1982, p. 210) that if women are more vulnerable to fusion (balance three), it is also possible that they are more capable of intimacy (balance five). And if men find it easier to reach psychological autonomy (balance four)—not to be confused with maturity—it is also possible that they find it harder to evolve to mature mutuality and relational interdependence (balance five).

Lastly, this method of counseling always contextualizes the individual in two ways. Initially it reminds us that a person is continually settling and resettling the issue of precisely what is the self and the other; the relationship between the individual and the social is made and remade at each balance. Also, it presumes that each of us is always in some culture of embeddedness that promotes or inhibits our development of maturity according to the way it *confirms* certain of our attitudes and actions, *contradicts* others, and *stays put* to allow us to reintegrate it into the new meaning of our self and others. As the biblical vision always sees the person in the context of the community of faith that hinders or supports spiritual growth, so this method of pastoral counseling aims to join the person in his or her concrete culture of embeddedness.

The significance of Kegan's model of maturity will be extended, in the next chapter, to include not only pastoral counseling but also spiritual direction. There the relationship of human maturity and Christian spirituality can be seen concretely in the practice of these two ministries. As this chapter focused on stage three in Kegan's developmental model, so the next chapter will explore case studies of more mature adults.

References

The Collected Works of St. Teresa of Avila. Vol. 2. Translated by Kieran Kavanaugh, O.C.D. and Otilio Rodriguez, O.C.D. Washington, D.C.: ICS Publications, 1980.

Keane, Philip S., S.S. *Sexual Morality: A Catholic Perspective.* New York: Paulist, 1977.

Kegan, Robert. *The Evolving Self.* Cambridge, MA: Harvard University Press, 1982.

Larkin, Ernest. *Silent Presence: Discernment as Process and Problem.* Denville, N.J.: Dimension Books, 1981.

Miller, Jean Baker. *Toward A New Psychology of Women.* Boston: Beacon, 1976.

Parks, Sharon. *The Critical Years.* San Francisco: Harper & Row, 1986.

Pruyser, Paul. *The Minister as Diagnostician.* Philadelphia: Westminster, 1976.

Rahner, Karl. *Foundations of Christian Faith.* New York: Seabury, 1978.

Schneiders, Sandra M. *Women and the Word.* New York: Paulist, 1986.

Steckel, Clyde J. "Directions in Pastoral Counseling." In *Clinical Handbook of Pastoral Counseling,* edited by Robert J. Wicks, Richard D. Parsons, and Donald E. Capps. New York: Paulist, 1985.

Wehr, Demaris S. *Jung & Feminism: Liberating Archetypes.* Boston: Beacon, 1987.

Chapter 5

Spiritual Direction and Pastoral Counseling: Similarities and Differences (Studies of More Mature Adults)

The way Christian spirituality relates to human maturity is seen, concretely, in the practice of spiritual direction and pastoral counseling. Most practitioners would agree with Barry and Connolly (1982) that spiritual direction is a process carried out in the context of a one-to-one relationship in which a competent guide helps a fellow Christian to grow in the spiritual life by means of personal encounters that have the directee's spiritual growth as their explicit object. Direction, in this situation, refers not to what the spiritual guide does; rather, it is the direction of God's spirit in the life of the directee that is discerned by the directee, with the help of the person whom tradition has referred to as the "spiritual director." In the past, directors have seen the relationship as a hierarchical one of authority over the directee, but theological evaluation of this attitude shows it to be an aberration. Pastoral counselors do not have such agreement on the nature of their pastoral ministry. As Orlo Strunk, Jr. notes in *Clinical Handbook of Pastoral Counseling* (1985, pp. 14–15), definitions range from the general "counseling done by a pastor or religious professional" to the official definition of the association which accredits this field: "a process in which a pastoral counselor utilizes insights and principles derived from the disciplines of theology and the behavioral sciences in working with individuals, couples, families, groups, and social systems toward the achievement of wholeness and health." Clearly, spiritual direction deals primarily with spirituality, while a survey of pastoral counseling texts demonstrates that in this ministry attention is focused primarily on human maturity, viewed from the controlling perspective of religious faith.

Both ministries realize their need for greater clarity about the other, complementary, dimension of their discipline. Pastoral counseling, which developed out of a Protestant tradition that was suspicious of spiritual direction because it was viewed as undermining the role of Christ as sole mediator, as not biblical, and as intrinsically hierarchical, now is not only admitting that this judgment is inaccurate but also turning to Catholic and Episcopal experts in spirituality in order to learn from them this practical and theoretical discipline. Moreover, Clinebell, in his newest edition (1984) of this widely used text in the field of pastoral counseling, maintains that spiritual healing and growth are the central tasks of this ministry. Despite this goal, Clinebell states that the explicit theological issues are the presenting problem in only a small minority of those seeking pastoral counseling. Those seeking spiritual direction, on the other hand, are all explicitly interested in spiritual growth, yet seldom present their situation as "a problem." Usually they speak of a "yearning" or "longing" for greater understanding of and deeper commitment to God's presence in their lives. Nevertheless, competent spiritual guides, realizing that God's presence affects us through the normal dynamics of our human nature, value the behavioral sciences, especially psychology.

Spiritual direction's desire to gain a more professional understanding of human maturity is demonstrated, for example, by inclusion of courses in psychology in its training programs and the popularity among spiritual directors of the journal *Human Development* which is dedicated to the integration of religion and psychology.

This chapter aims to clarify the reciprocal and inseparable relationship of Christian spirituality and human maturity by examining the relationship of these ministries which deal primarily with either side of that relationship. By means of the stories of two persons seeking pastoral care, the chapter will (1) explain the common ground shared by spiritual guides and pastoral counselors; (2) distinguish each ministry's specific angle of vision and principles for proceeding onto that common ground.

Stories of Ellen and Bill

A. *Ellen Seeks Spiritual Direction from Joan*

Ellen's story is based directly on a description given in Carolyn Gratton's *Trusting* (1982). The interpretation of Ellen's story and the case study of her relationship to Joan, her spiritual director, are my own creative illustration of the issues in this chapter. Using Kegan's model of maturity and principles from classical sources in spirituality (e.g. scripture, Teresa of Avila, Ignatius of Loyola) Joan will demonstrate this book's thesis regarding the correlation of spirituality and personal maturity.

Ellen's story (c.f. Gratton, 1982, pp. 12, 114–115). Ellen, a single woman in her mid-thirties, enjoys her demanding work in a hospice for persons dying of cancer. After a brief affair with an older man with whom she worked, she discovered she was pregnant. At first she panicked. Then in prayerful reflection she realized that she believed in God's providence. To Ellen, this means that wherever she is, whatever she has done, that is precisely where the road to heaven begins. However she may have complicated her journey, the Lord still "waits to be gracious" to her (Is 30:18). She decided to trust God, to move into the unknown, to have the baby. She then sought help from Joan, a competent spiritual guide, in order to discern more fully how to deepen her relationship to God in this situation. As Ellen narrated her experience to Joan she wondered, "In a crisis at work I always manage to stay together; yet here I was, falling apart. Could it be that 'not having all my ducks in a row' was giving God an opportunity to intervene in my life?"

Their conversation will continue below.

Bill Seeks Pastoral Counseling from Don

Bill's story is described in Donald Capps' article, "Pastoral Counseling for Middle Adults" (1985) Here also, the interpre-

tation of Bill's problem and the description of Don's relationship to him as a pastoral counselor are my own creation and
function as an illustration of the issues in this chapter. Don, like
Joan in the other case, will have Kegan's perspective on human
maturity and this will shape the way he decides to help Bill with
his presenting problem.

*Bill's Initial Conversation with His Pastor (Capps, pp. 232–
234)*

Bill Harris has been dominating and overpowering his wife
and children. Bill's wife, Arlene, accepted his domineering
ways. But when they both reached forty, she decided that she
could no longer tolerate him and threatened to file for divorce.
When he came to the stark realization that she really meant it,
Bill called their pastor and asked him for an appointment with
the two of them.

Bill: Yesterday she filed for divorce. I don't want it. I want
her. She says she doesn't love me, but I don't believe this.
We've been married fifteen years. People don't stay married
that long if there isn't something there. I don't understand her
attitude. I've been a responsible husband and father all along.
What am I doing that's wrong?

Arlene: It's not that you do anything. There just isn't anything there. I can't say anything without his twisting it all
around. He's so hard on our daughter. He makes her feel this
high.

Bill: Somebody's got to discipline the girl! You don't!
You'd just let her run wild.

Pastor [Don]: You feel she's too permissive with your
daughter?

Bill: Well, wouldn't you want to know where your daughter is at all times—especially with all that's going on in our city
streets?

Pastor [Don]: You mean you are justified in feeling the way
you do?

Bill: You're just like my wife. You keep trying to put it back on me. I wish you would tell me what she really expects of me. She won't even tell me what she doesn't like about me.

The pastor proceeded to point out that Arlene appears to be tired of being continually squelched. Significantly, Bill accepts this judgment and asks whether it would help their marriage if he tried to change this. But Arlene is unconvinced that Bill really wants to change. Moreover, she confesses that she is simply tired of the fighting.

Arlene: You're more clever with words and arguments than I am, and you know it. So what are we trying to prove, that you are always right? I just can't live with this kind of tension all the time?

Bill: Of course I am not always right—that's absurd! But I try to be responsible. I don't drink and carouse around.

Arlene: You, you are "Mr. Pure and Right."

Their conversation will continue below.

Spiritual Direction and Pastoral Counseling

Spiritual direction and pastoral counseling have five characteristics in common. Within each of these there are principles or methods that I believe are unique to spiritual direction. Each characteristic will be explained and then illustrated through the stories of either Ellen or Bill.

1. A Working Alliance

Common to both counselors and spiritual guides is their involvement in a working alliance which will go against another person's well-defended personality. Secular counselors would interpret the source of that alliance simply as the human drive toward life and growth, or as the tendency toward self-actualization or the will-to-health. Both pastoral counselors and spiritual guides would agree with their secular colleagues as far as they go, yet would extend the interpretation to include its ultimate source: the indwelling Spirit of the living God who desires that we experience life abundantly. The life force and the Source of this life are absolutely inseparable. In other words, grace builds on and permeates nature. In seeking an ultimate source for this drive to life, in appreciating it, and in counting on it, pastoral counselors and spiritual guides have still more common ground. Those approaching these ministries differ in their direct attention to this ultimate source. Whereas those seeking pastoral counseling seldom pay explicit and consistent attention to the theological dimension of their alliance, those approaching spiritual direction always pay explicit and consistent attention to God's presence.

Bill seeks counseling from his pastor regarding his collapsing marriage because he and Arlene were married in church and they associate marriage with religious teaching about fidelity and permanence. In spite of the fact that counseling will involve exposure of his failures, Bill and Don form a working alliance based on Bill's desire to heal this wound in his life even though the remedy is painful. Arlene is also an important person in this particular working alliance. However, for the sake of focus and a balance of women's (Ellen) and men's experience, Bill will receive primary, though not exclusive attention.

Like Bill, Ellen is willing to endure the discomfort of exposing her weakness in order to form a working alliance with a person who will help her grow in understanding and love. Unlike Bill, she seeks first to experience, with understanding and commitment, the presence of God in her current situation. All other aspects of her life are perceived from this vantage point.

2. Mutual Contract or Agreement Regarding (a) What the Client/Directee Wants; (b) What the Counselor/Guide Can Do

Both counselors and guides make a mutual agreement or contract regarding what their client or directee wants and what they as the counselor or guide can do. As this objective is examined the unique aspect of each ministry emerges; for what the directee wants differs in several ways from the client's desires, and the counselor's competence usually differs from that of a spiritual guide.

(a) What the Directee or Client Wants

a.1. Relationship with God or problem solving. Ellen seeks guidance in deepening her relationship to God, while Bill desires help in order to see and solve a problem.

In both ministries the "presenting objective" may require evaluation. Someone may seek spiritual direction, for example, as a substitute for counseling because he cannot admit that he might have psychological problems. Or another person might approach this ministry in order to please religious authorities or because it is the "in thing to do" and be unable to benefit from it because she does not yet really want to face the demands of personal prayer. On the other hand, one may seek pastoral counseling presuming that the counselor is competent to help with contemplative prayer. Yet few pastoral counselors have received the long-term spiritual direction that would fit them to give the ministry of spiritual direction, so they would likely refer a person to a guide who could help her or him meet her or his objective.

a.2. Surrender to God; autonomy and its limits. In spiritual direction, a mature adult wants to affirm her or his autonomy yet move beyond the limits of autonomy in order to surrender to God. Because most believers perceive surrender and union with God as the dominant themes of religion, they are often suspicious of their feelings of adult autonomy. They assume these must be relinquished completely in order to grow in faith. They are unfamiliar with the way scripture and classical writings in spirituality validate the human longings for independence and non-conformity as much as they affirm the longing for relationship and connection. Ellen, for example, realizes the value of "staying together," of being in control of her life. Unlike Elizabeth (in Chapter 4) for whom self-assertion felt uncomfortable and associated with "guilt," Ellen has the maturity which allows her to feel at home with being self-directed. At the same time, she wisely perceives the limitations of this "having her ducks in a row." The primacy in her life of religious values such as charity and mutual support have enabled Ellen to consider the positive opportunities present in a situation in which she cannot control every aspect of her life. From the beginning of her alliance with Joan, then, Ellen senses the limits of autonomy as a goal of maturity. Present also, however, is a tinge of suspicion about autonomy itself. Ellen's language about the way God is present is the language of "intervention" which usually connotes one-sided control rather than mutuality, of movement from the outside in. She has doubts that she can have adult control and be in deep relationship to God. This will be an important topic for her conversation with Joan. At the same time, the fact that her primary goal is religious, and therefore relationship with God and others, enables Ellen to realize the limits of autonomy.

Bill, on the other hand, has no such awareness of the limits of autonomy. As an adult, he has strong self-control and a healthy ability to satisfy some basic needs. Having become fixed or overdefended in the evolutionary balance of stereotypically male qualities, however, he creates the meaning of himself primarily through control of relationships and work. He shows no awareness of the constraining isolation that commingles with strong independence. In contrast, his wife Arlene is only now becoming aware of the limitations of her embeddedness in relationships to Bill and to their daughter, and is in the early phase of evolving into a self who has independence, who has some distance, and therefore some ability to criticize the destructive aspects of her fusion with Bill. She is exhausted by the effort it is taking to be responsible for her own preferences and to endure Bill's unwillingness and inability to give up any control in their relationship. The effort to elicit mutuality from Bill is so great that she is tempted simply to quit.

Relationship to God may be inseparable from Bill's and Arlene's primary goal of a better marriage, but it is not identical with it. Their objective is human maturity: a more mature marriage partnership. Ellen will, no doubt, wrestle with the same longings for independence and union that Bill and Arlene have, yet in Ellen's case these are examined insofar as they affect her primary objective: deepening her response to God's presence. Of course, Ellen and Bill may each implicitly seek what the other desires. But the explicit focus differs for each person.

(b) *What the Spiritual Guide or Counselor Can Do*

b.1. Clarify what the person really wants. Like the counselor, the guide first of all clarifies what the person who comes to her really wants. For example, if one wants adult surrender to God, the guide realizes that one must also want—or learn to want—the self-direction and autonomy that are the prerequisites of authentic self-surrender. Women, especially, can be very unclear about their basic desires. Because women are socialized to notice and respond to everyone else's desires, they frequently repress their own desires so much that they do not or cannot easily contact them. Or they cannot admit a longing for autonomy because they assume it means selfishness or self-centeredness. On the other hand, women like Ellen will sometimes resist autonomy because they wisely suspect it is not the appropriate goal of human or spiritual maturity. What is detrimental for women—their embeddedness in relationships—can also generate something positive: appreciation for the way attachment and belonging are just as valuable for human growth as differentiation and autonomy.

What is significant for both men and women is noticing and evaluating their basic desires. Counselors' training in the dominant psychological theories, which identify maturity with autonomy, can inhibit their ability to clarify clients' desires to move beyond autonomy. Spiritual guides, on the other hand, trained to value self-sacrifice, must be alert to examine what can easily appear to be religious charity but can actually be immature immersion in others' lives. To praise persons like Elizabeth (in Chapter 4) who spend their lives on others, who defer to others' needs, who do not express justified anger, can actually retard their religious development. Persons like these must develop their self-coherence in order to donate an authentic self to God and to others. Spiritual guides may unintentionally reinforce immaturity when they use religious insights divorced from approriate psychological theory.

Because spirituality and maturity are inseparable, the immaturity reinforced here is both religious and psychological. Both counselor and guide also look for religious delusions or pathology which are, unlike genuine religious experience, compensatory and extremely self-serving. Joan, for example, would be alert to the possibility that Ellen might, in religious matters, want to deny personal power through enforced passivity. Don would be alert to the possibility that Bill legitimates his domineering ways by involving biblical "teaching" on male headship and women's subordination.

b.2. No conflicting loyalties. Like the counselor, the guide acts without conflicting loyalties. Spiritual direction is not "used" to keep a person in the seminary or in an unhappy marriage, nor is counseling an appropriate vehicle for promoting the counselor's own moral values.

b.3. Difference in the use of the working alliance relationship. In contrast to the counselor, the guide does not directly use the relationship with the directee in order to achieve the goal of their conversations. In psychodynamic terms, transference is not fostered or used therapeutically. Some transference and countertransference are inevitable, but are noticed and evaluated in terms of the criterion of the relationship: be a guiding sister or brother, in Christ, to the directee, not a therapist or spiritual parent. (This theme is developed in section b.6. below.) The guide/directee relationship is completely subordinate (though significant) to the primary relationship attended to in their conversations: the directee's relationship to God, in Christ Jesus, by the power of the Spirit. That relationship to God is absolutely inseparable from the directee's everyday relationship to herself and to everyone else—all of which are topics of conversation in direction—but the faith relationship is not reduced to those other relationships and is not entirely the product of those relationships. (There will be more about this in the next section.) Without a vision of faith and without personal experience of seeking God in personal prayer and surrender of heart one cannot grasp the distinction

I am making here. What helps to draw out this distinction most sharply, perhaps, is the contrast between what the guide and counselor are *primarily* doing in each session.

b.4. Primary task. Primarily, the counselor is using his human maturity (i.e. freedom from self-preoccupation, loving concern for the client, the fruit of his own struggles for integrated self-awareness) to facilitate the client's own insights and self-direction concerning his experience of making the meaning of himself and others represented by the problem he presents. The spiritual guide, on the other hand, is primarily surrendering herself to God. She is giving herself to Holy Wisdom so that her religious maturity (i.e. her ability to surrender to God free of compulsion and conformity, capacity for intimacy with God and others, experience of the way God directs and empowers her and others, personal "verification" of the teaching of scripture and the saints, detachment from self-image, ability to act without seeking the fruit of her action, fidelity to personal and communal prayer, freedom from self-preoccupation and intrusive curiosity) can be a revelation of life as an adult daughter of God our divine parent, that is, of life "in Christ." Joan loves Ellen as Jesus, the Christ, has loved Joan (Jn 15:12). She primarily aims to be the free, struggling, flexible, humanly involved "instrument" for helping the directee notice and respond to God's directing presence in every aspect of her life.

b.5. Primary attitude. Don's inner attitude, then, is primarily active in order to join Bill and Arlene in the way that Don judges can assist them to make the choice to do the work of human growth. Don must also be receptive, be a "guest" insofar as he must wait and seek Bill's and Arlene's verification that he grasps their experience accurately. But the primary attitude, for Don, is active; it is energetic attention to what he should say and do in order to facilitate Bill's and Arlene's work on their problematic relationship. Joan, on the other hand, is primarily attentive to God's presence, in Ellen's life (and in her own). Like Don, Joan also actively joins another person in her experience. But here the nature of the experience she joins is quite different from Bill's relationship to Arlene. Indeed, it is the experience of a relationship to God who permeates Ellen's life in ways that move invisibly unless we know how to "read the signs," and—especially in a religiously mature person like Ellen—"gently, as when a drop of water soaks into a sponge" (Ignatius of Loyola), and in ways that are "extremely subtle and delicate, and almost imperceptible" (John of the Cross). Therefore, in contrast to Don whose receptivity is in the service of assisting persons to set their own agenda for doing the work that human growth demands, Joan and Ellen avoid setting any agenda of their own and devote their active receptivity to experiencing with understanding and commitment God's "agenda," that is, God's empowering presence in Ellen's life.

b.6. Primary relationship. Joan's relationship to Ellen is not a professional "role" as a (spiritual) counselor; nor is she her spiritual mother. Rather her relationship is one of acting out a specifically Christian relationship, namely that of her sister in Christ.

As Sandra Schneiders explains in *Spiritual Direction* (1977, pp. 47–48), the New Testament specifies the revelation of the Hebrew bible on the subject of spiritual relationships in several ways. First, the parental relationship of God to us becomes literal and specific, while remaining spiritual. It is no longer a metaphorical expression of creation which emphasizes the personal and gratuitous quality of God's creative love for us. Rather, God, who is revealed as the real, non-patriarchal father of the divine Son, has become in truth our parent, engendering us by the Spirit to a real participation in the filiation of Jesus, in the divine life itself. Second, the fraternal/sororal relationship among the members of the people of God is no longer based on blood ties or even common belonging to the covenant. Rather, we have become brothers and sisters by a new title: participation in the filiation of Jesus (Jn 1:12, 20:17).

This revelation has important implications for the spiritual direction relationship, as Schneiders also notes. First it is based and modeled upon the relationship in the Spirit between Jesus and us. We love one another as he has loved us (Jn 13:34–35).

Second, our love of others is always essentially fraternal or sororal and is a manifestation of the inner mystery of God. As Jesus showed us the Father by being perfect Son and Brother, so we, by living our filial relationship to God and our fraternal or sororal relationship to one another, manifest the parental mystery of God (Jn 14:8–11). Third, the gospel commands us to imitate our heavenly Father in order to live as God's children, not in order to exercise God's paternity toward one another (Mt 23:8–9). Lastly, the literal word for child is reserved for the Christian in relation to God or to the Christian community. Even Paul, who calls Christians his "children," nuances this usage by telling them to be imitators of him as he is of Christ. Thus, it is not the role of God, source of the spiritual life, which Paul assumes toward his converts, but the role of Christ, Son and Brother. The analogy Paul evokes is simply that between physical parenthood and pastoral care, that which other biblical authors convey by using the Greek word which means "child" in a metaphorical or adoptive sense, not a literal sense.

Now we can see the practical consequences for Joan's attitude and action in the spiritual direction relationship. First, it is always and essentially a sororal one. There are times when she will be called upon to teach or even to confront Ellen with firmness. But there is a very real difference between being an older or more experienced sister and being a parent. The guide who thinks of herself (or himself) as "manifesting God's will" is falsifying the relationship. We have one divine parent, and God has not deputized anyone, not even Jesus, to assume that role.

Second, the sororal relationship is one of essential equality which admits only to temporary or circumstantial inequalities (e.g. of theological learning or spiritual gifts). Therefore, Joan's attitude is always one of mutuality, respect, familial friendship, as well as self-sacrificing love. She always fosters Ellen's initiative, and trusts her with responsibility. She manifests to Ellen her awareness of their common participation in and responsibility for the family life of God which they share in the Spirit and show forth to the world. In other words, Joan's most important activity is to show Ellen what it means to be an adult daughter of God. She does this by the wholehearted way that she serves Ellen's life. Ellen, in turn, as she experiences more and more deeply her own identity as a daughter, will come to know the true God who is Mother and Father, the only source of our life.

Don, too, is a real brother, in Christ, to Bill and Arlene. What they seek from Don, however, is not a relationship that focuses primarily on this Christian relationship which they share. Rather, they want a relationship permeated by Don's competence as a professional counselor with skills that Bill and Arlene need in order to see and solve their problem.

b.7. Different training. Spiritual directors are trained to facilitate spiritual discernment: understanding and responding to God's presence in one's life. This requires that spiritual directors be in spiritual direction themselves, manifest the call to this ministry by being sought as a spiritual guide (without having "hung out a shingle" to advertise this service and without having presumed that the ability came automatically with ordination), have competence in the theological discipline of spirituality (as explained in Chapter 1), and undergo supervision of their experience of being sought out by others to be a spiritual guide.

Spiritual guides are also trained to promote spiritual maturity, which means development beyond autonomy to the balance of independence and relationship that allows genuine intimacy with God and others. This requires an understanding of the psychology of personality and a working knowledge of its relationship to faith development. Training for this type of pastoral care, then, integrates psychology and the special theological discipline of spirituality, with the primary focus being on spirituality.

Pastoral counselors, too, integrate psychology and theology, but with primary emphasis on psychology. Their theological training follows the guidelines of requirements for the master of divinity degree which is designed to prepare people to preach, celebrate liturgy, teach theology to non-professionals, corrdinate the ministries of a church, and do beginning level counseling from a pastoral perspective. Their psychological training may be as little as one or two courses in the M.Div. Curriculum, or as much as a graduate degree in counseling psychology. The focus of integration, for most pastoral counselors, is that of biblical theology correlated with developmental psychology.

I believe that new points of convergence are emerging in these two fields. Some Protestant theologians, whose tradition has been wary of mysticism, asceticism, and other aspects of what is now called the discipline of spirituality, are doing two important things that converge with the Catholic and Anglican tradition of spiritual direction. They are developing a field of "practical theology" that bears some resemblance to the way spiritual direction traditions have attempted to understand what both groups might call the "logic of divine-human interaction." And, second, some are rediscovering their roots in movements of Protestant "piety." For example, faculty and divinity students at Southern Methodist University have adapted John Wesley's directives for sustaining and evaluating Christian life to their life as a community of present and future ministers.

More direct convergence is manifest among a few pastoral counselors who want to focus the entire process on counseling for faith development, or on assisting sanctification as a process, or on correlating depth psychotherapy with religious development. These practitioners are, I believe, attempting to redefine what pastoral counseling has traditionally been in order to transform it into what spiritual direction has always been. That is, they want to give primary attention to explicitly religious issues, to one's experience of God, and to view psychological issues as aspects of life which hinder or help the quality of one's relation to God.

3. Facilitate a Process of Sharing Inner States

The inseparability and reciprocity of Christian spirituality and human maturity are most evident when we examine this third area of common ground shared by counselors and spiritual guides. Both facilitate another person's process of sharing inner states. In both counseling and direction, thoughts and feelings are noticed, described and evaluated. In both ministries there is a formal process involving the strenuous work of self-knowledge and self-acceptance.

(a) *Sharing religious experience* The guide facilitates the process which Christian spirituality names discernment. Christian discernment of the Spirit's gentle guidance in the directee's life is possible only through an examination of the inner (psychological) states which motivate and permeate action. For it is in "the secrets of the heart" that God's presence and guidance are revealed. Christian tradition is unanimous on this point. God's guidance is present in many other ways, for example in historical events and the prophetic action of the community; but, in the last analysis, it must be one's own understanding and judgment that decides whether this event or that person is a manifestation of God's guidance. Anything less is reverting to magic, an abdication of conscience, an immature conformity to authority, a distortion of the biblical call to "listen" and freely allow oneself to be converted.

Sharing one's deepest feelings and thoughts as they occur in prayer is often the focus of conversation in spiritual direction. Every other aspect of life is attended to also, but it is noticed insofar as it mirrors or affects one's relationship to God.

God's presence and guidance emerge in Ellen's consciousness in direction as she shares the four aspects of prayer which Barry and Connolly describe (1982, pp. 69–79): noticing my feeling-response to life situations; how I express this to God, Jesus, the Spirit; how I listen for God's response to my expression of feeling; how I express my response to God's being this way toward me.

Ellen tells Joan how she felt about her brief affair with Harry and the discovery that she was pregnant.

Ellen: I felt so comfortable with Harry, so trusting, so sure that deep down he really loved me and wanted an intimate relationship with me but wasn't sure himself how to have this kind of relationship with a younger woman. He was a bit surprised, I think, that I was so sexually attracted to him and was so at ease with the idea of sleeping with him. I took precautions against getting pregnant but this was one of those cases where it didn't work. When I discovered I was pregnant I panicked, at first. My first thoughts were the sort of teenage response: What will people think? Will Harry think I've tried to trap him into marriage? What will this do to my family and my career? But my second thoughts were mainly about Harry and me and the baby. This was something I could not control; I just accidentally got pregnant and now Harry and I would have to discuss the situation calmly. At the hospital we had worked together on situations that were tougher than this, I thought. I was really naive! Those situations did not concern us; they were always about someone else's life and death situation. Harry was shocked that I was pregnant; he was immediately thinking about how it would interfere with his independence and how impossible it was for him to begin again as a father at his age (he is a widower with teenaged children); he was unable to discuss these feelings. Whatever I wanted to do about the baby, he said, was fine with him and he would give me some financial help, but he could not handle fathering an infant. Frankly, I was confused and surprised at his response. I know how to handle people's response at hearing that they were dying of cancer, but I didn't know how to handle this.

Joan: This must have been very confusing and have hurt you, Ellen. You said earlier that you brought this situation to God in prayer. How did you do that?

Ellen: After Harry left my apartment that night, I just sat in bed and cried and prayed, "Where are you, Lord? Why can't I love somebody and have it work? I know better than to think that getting pregnant is punishment for being a 'bad girl,' but I don't know where you are or what to do!"

Joan: How did God feel to you as you prayed this way, Ellen?

Ellen: How did God feel? Interesting question. I never thought about it just that way. Well, I guess God felt far away, absent, at first.

Joan: You say "at first."

Ellen: Yes, it was only at first that God seemed far away. My experience with dying patients has confirmed my faith in God's providence. No matter where people have wandered in their lives, no matter what they have done, I have seen them begin to experience God "waiting to be gracious" to them. I have become convinced that if I "abide in love," as John's gospel says, Jesus dwells in me and I in him, and somehow things will work out.

Joan: So you felt, after all, that God was waiting to be gracious to you, and that somehow Jesus dwells in you, especially when you are loving.

Ellen: Exactly, and I knew in my heart that I was honestly loving Harry. So I really thanked God that I had this ability to love and trust even though Harry didn't know how to respond to it. I wanted to make Harry listen, to make him understand, to take control the way I do at the hospital. But he isn't a dying patient so he could get up and leave. And he did. Then I began to think that this lack of control may be just the way God is now able to intervene in my life. Now that "all my ducks aren't in a row" God can finally really get into *my* life the way he does with my patients.

Joan: Ellen, you say that God feels gracious and present to you, especially in and through love. And you talk about lack of control as the thing that lets God get into your life in a special way. Is that correct?

Ellen: Yes, that's it.

Joan: Earlier, Ellen, you talked about the satisfaction that you feel in being competent at the hospital, in being self-directed, as it were. Now you were saying that it's lack of control that connects you to God. Please help me to understand better how these two feelings are present in your life now."

This segment of a conversation in spiritual direction illustrates some of the basic connections between prayer and the rest of life and it reveals the way Joan is using principles from classical sources in spirituality. Teresa of Avila, for example, in

The Interior Castle teaches that self-knowledge is essential for growth in prayer. No matter how many years one has given to personal prayer and no matter how "advanced" one is in contemplative prayer, she teaches, one never loses the need for greater self-knowledge. Joan's conversations with Ellen are designed to help her with this process. Another classical source, Ignatius of Loyola, in his *Spiritual Exercises*, which give detailed guidelines for the discernment of God's presence, advises one to pay primary attention to one's feelings. Joan is phrasing her comments and questions in ways that keep feeling in the forefront of their mutual attention. Clearly, these spiritual writers assume that prayer and all of life are intrinsically connected, and Ellen's narrative confirms this connection.

A few examples can clarify this basic connection. As Ellen responds to humans who hurt her, so does she respond to the Source of life if "life has hurt her." She responds to Harry's rejection by trying to understand him, by relating this negative experience to the rest of her life which she sees as also full of satisfaction. So she responds to God by trusting her past experience of God and trying to understand how this fits into the wider picture. If her creation of the meaning of herself were so dependent and fused with others that Ellen was preoccupied with defending herself from being hurt by their rejection, then she would tend to defend herself (often unconsciously) from relationship with God who might also reject her. This is not the case, though, for Ellen has an adult sense of self-direction and an adult ability to relate to those whom she may lose (her dying patients, for example). She is convinced of the limits of autonomy as the criteria for maturity as she manifests in her realization that "lack of control" in life might be an opportunity for a new awareness of God (learned, again, from her hospice patients), and her realization that Harry's fear of interference with his independent life style is not mature. Thus, she connects God's special presence in her life with a situation in which she lacks autonomy. An accidental pregnancy could be the occasion for God's "intervention."

Joan is helping Ellen clarify this image of God, this feeling that God somehow "prefers" situations when people are not in

control of their life. This is important for Ellen's discernment
of God's presence and for Ellen's ability to progress in adult
faith. As I have explained in more detail elsewhere (1980, p.
298), if one is developing a sense of herself or himself as free
and self-directed, then she or he must relate to a God who
affirms and empowers that freedom if she or he is to preserve
that self-identity. If Ellen's prior religious education or experience provided only an image of God who prefers child-like
dependence and who acts principally by intruding from the
outside in, then Ellen will either sustain her current sense of an
independent adult who relates lovingly to others on an adult
basis and eventually "reject God" (i.e. the only God she
knows), or compartmentalize her prayer by repressing in
prayer the adult feelings she manifests in the rest of her life, or
somehow try to reconcile these conflicting images. Joan's experience and training have already alerted her to the conflicting
feelings and images in Ellen's narrative and Joan wants immediately to help Ellen keep attending to the full range of feeling
present in her experience of God. Lack of self-knowledge here
could hinder Ellen's discernment of the "real" God beyond her
projections and result in unresolved developmental issues—
religious and human developmental issues. For a free adult self
cannot be intimate with a paternalistic or maternalistic God,
that is with a God who treats adults like children. On the other
hand, appreciation of adult self-direction is difficult for a deeply
prayerful person like Ellen if she suspects that such a stance is
somehow "contrary to God's will" or not as pleasing to God as
is passivity and lack of control.

Joan wants to help Ellen clarify her experience of longing
to surrender to God. Does the "lack of control" that Ellen
rightly discerns as an opportunity for deeper relationship to
God refer to the passivity of child-like dependence or to the
adult willingness to let go of one's legitimate ability to direct
one's life independently in order to receive another's self-communication and live in mutuality and union of wills? In other
words, is surrender regression to fusion with the dominant will
of another, or is it a movement that subsumes autonomy into a
relationship of intimacy? Part of this discernment process will

include suggesting that Ellen identify other experiences that she judges to be experiences of God's presence. Joan will assist Ellen to correlate these with biblical revelation of God's Spirit as empowering. Sharing religious experience in this discernment process enables Joan and Ellen to see the reciprocal relationship between spirituality and personal maturity.

(b) Sharing the experience of struggling for human maturity (in a Christian context). At mid-life, Bill is surprised to see his wife and daughter moving away from him. His wife says she wants a divorce and his teenage daughter wants to do things without always asking her parents. Don, Bill's pastor, responds to Bill's request for help.

Don: How are you feeling about all of this, Bill?

Bill: Confused, believe me! I don't understand what they want me to do—just let our daughter run wild? Just let Arlene's working and taking classes interfere with our family life and with my business plans?

Don: So, you feel that your life is very disorderly and messed up.

Bill: You bet it is! But it's worse than that, Don. It's downright wrong. I'm responsible for taking care of my wife and daughter, and how am I supposed to do that when Arlene keeps interfering when I correct Marlene? Now Arlene says she doesn't love me. But I have killed myself to be a good provider and to give them everything I could afford and to be kind and patient. What more could I possibly do?

Don: You feel wronged.

Bill: Yes, I deserve better than this. How can they be impatient with me when I have gone out of my way for years to be considerate and to plan things so that they could be happy and contented?

Don: It sounds as if you feel very hurt and puzzled about what is happening in your family now.

Bill: Yeah, I guess "hurt" is a good way to describe it. Just between you and me, Don, I think I feel deserted, abandoned. I'm feeling as though I want something from Arlene that I'm not getting. And this is a feeling that I absolutely hate to have. It's the pits. When I have this feeling I find that I just move away from the person and think, "O.K., if that's how you're going to be, it's okay. I'll get along." So maybe I should just let her have her divorce. But she knows this is not what the Bible teaches about marriage. And she must know that I have been trying to be a responsible Christian man and head of our household.

Don hears two themes in Bill's conversation. First, he hears that Bill creates the meaning of himself as one who is in complete control of life. Bill's care and patience in relationships are aspects of his control of the relationships; he is the loving provider. Now, Arlene's affirmation of her own wishes, and her desire for separation, for independence, raises the most radical questions about the way Bill makes the meaning of himself. It is just beginning to dawn on Bill that creating the meaning of himself this way has costs. He is experiencing slight doubts about whether these costs are worth it. Before he can decide whether to choose the growth work that it would take to evolve into a new way of creating the meaning of himself, a self that would let go of control and receive Arlene's and Marlene's desires for mutuality with him as legitimate, Bill will resist mightily and mourn grievously the loss of a way of making meaning that his self has come to know as its entire self. It would not be meeting Bill in his experience if Don were to encourage Bill to develop the more "feminine" side of himself at mid-life, to be more receptive. The experience that Bill brings into counseling is one that represents precisely the problem of *not having* a receptive (stereotypically "feminine") side to develop. The only meaning of receptivity Don has is that of "compromising one's principles," of weakness. Don also hears Bill interpreting Christian themes in a manner that legitimates the way Bill makes the meaning of himself.

Hearing these two themes, Don will not only assist Bill to make the choice to grow psychologically, but will also help him to notice the way his interpretation of Christianity is acting as a barrier to his psychological maturity—that is, it now inhibits his capacity to move beyond autonomy to genuine intimacy. Bill's version of Christian teaching is reinforcing his socialization to be a workaholic and perfectionist because he concentrates on the force of "gospel demands," "God's discipline," and "Christian ideals." He is unaware of what Bernard Cooke (1983) explains is a "reversal of the patriarchal and hierarchical model of God's fatherhood." He lacks attention to what Roy Fairchild (1982) points out is a capacity for deeper identity because "Christ lives in me," and "God's intention can be realized through surrender of one's current self-definition."

In summary, both counselors and spiritual guides commit themselves to a parallel process of assisting persons to notice and interpret their inner feelings and thoughts so that they may overcome their defenses for the sake of deeper life. Because the Christian experience of God, in Christ and the Spirit, comes only through concrete human experience and culturally influenced symbols, Christian spirituality embraces every dimension of human thought and feeling, but is not reduced to them. God is, of course, beyond all limits, yet God touches us in our limitations. As Raymond Brown (1981) reminds us, there is no communication from God to us except through our human interpretation and expression of the revelatory insight from God that we call "the word of God." Whether that insight from God that is expressed in human terms be scripture, or historical decisions, or our own everyday lives, it is a matter of thoughts and feelings being expressed and interpreted. Both pastoral counselors and spiritual guides attend to these inner motions of the heart but from differing primary vantage points.

Counselors make concern for human maturity the perspective from which they see Christian spirituality, while guides see things the other way around. As a marriage counselor, Don attends to Bill's thoughts and feelings about Christianity insofar as they promote or inhibit his human maturity. Don helps Bill to notice that his patriarchal Christianity is preventing him from accepting his own human limitations and entering adult relationships with his wife and daughter. Joan, on the other hand, attends to Ellen's struggles for human maturity because they are inseparable from Ellen's manner of relating to God. Joan is convinced that Ellen's greater human maturity increases

Ellen's ability to perceive the "real" God who calls Ellen to be a friend, not a child.

Although pastoral counselors do *not focus the process* of counseling primarily and directly on a client's relationship to God, I believe that they can, nevertheless, directly promote that relationship. They do this in two ways. First, they do it insofar as they assist development beyond autonomy. For that capacity is at the very essence of authentic Christian spirituality. Without something of that capacity to risk intimacy, one's relationship to God is conformity, compulsion, or merely cultural religion. With that capacity one has a self and can surrender; indeed, the process of ever deeper surrender to God in all the complexities of life is the very definition of Christian holiness. Second, the counselor directly promotes the client's relationship to God insofar as he or she reinforces only a mature Christian vision, and does not cooperate with a retarded Christian vision which fears mutuality and seeks only security.

I mean by "mature Christianity" that persistent stream of teaching within the tradition which retains two convictions. First, it recognizes that human autonomy is legitimate and necessary for authentic self-donation and religious commitment. The theology of repentance, conversion, and discernment, for example, assumes that God invites free, self-directed persons to trust their own judgments about the authenticity of their religious experience and risk entering a loving relationship with God who cannot be manipulated and does not manipulate them. Second, it understands Christian surrender and union with God not as loss of self but as complete mutuality with differentiation. Union with God does involve loss of self-image. However, Christian contemplatives distinguish this self-image from the "true self" which one is and remains even in the mystical prayer of union with a personal God.

4. Deal with Defenses—Habitual Ways of Coping with Life That Function as Protection for Feelings That Are Threatened, as Safeguards Against Vulnerability

(a) *Religion as a defense.* Before discussing "defense mechanisms," in general, it is worth noting that both counselors and guides expect that the persons they talk with may use religion itself as a defense. That is, religion may be used to legitimate avoidance of the effort it takes to have honest, deep relationships. Involvement with a charismatic prayer group, for example, may lead a person to present his or her needs and desires as what "God told me to do," or what "God wants me to tell you." This defense against the struggles involved in persuading people to agree with one's plans or point of view may be obvious to the spiritual guide but unconscious for the directee. Intense involvement with parish activities may not be generous service but, rather, escape from facing the difficulties of marriage to an insensitive or abusive spouse. The client may not see that activity is not necessarily good just because it is religious; indeed immature religious activity may be more problematic than other behavior because more subject to illusion and more carefully defended.

(b) Defense against the threatened way of making the meaning of oneself. Bill's response to his experience of a troubled marriage demonstrates his habitual way of defending himself against the vulnerability involved in relationships that are mutual and intimate. He ignored the signals from his wife that said she wanted to relate to him as a partner rather than as a subordinate. He refuses to believe that his wife could really mean to leave him. He rationalizes, talking about the moralistic reasons why he is right to maintain control over his wife and daughter.

Once, however, he tells Don how he feels. Bill says that he feels that he needs something from Arlene and he hates having this feeling. This is Don's opening to begin helping Bill to notice that he is defending himself and to begin exploring what it is that he is defending and why he defends it.

(c) Defense against relating realistically to God. Unlike Bill's situation in pastoral counseling where he defends himself in his conversations with Don, Ellen's resistance does not show up very much in her sessions with her guide, Joan. Rather, it is in Ellen's prayer that she demonstrates defensiveness. As Joan

listens to Ellen describe her new awareness of her own religious experience in prayer, Joan hears some clues that might be seen as God's invitation to a deeper relationship that Ellen may be resisting. Don's understanding of Bill's defensiveness comes primarily from studying theories of personality and Don's experience as a pastoral counselor. Joan's sensitivity to Ellen's defenses comes primarily from Joan's own experience of being in spiritual direction herself and noticing her own patterns of defense, from prayerful reflection on the autobiographical writing of persons struggling for intimacy with God (Teresa of Avila and Thomas Merton, for example), from awareness of defenses typical of stages in life-span development, and from her prayerful attention to God's Spirit as she listens to Ellen speak about longing to relate honestly and intimately to God.

After many sessions of relaxed, candid, sisterly conversation about Ellen's times of quiet prayer and experiences of God's empowering presence as Ellen relates to her dying patients, Joan and Ellen begin to notice some patterns of Ellen's resistance or defense. The defenses they are interested in are those that emerge in Ellen's prayer. Ellen feels that her new ability to notice the defenses is itself the fruit of prayer. That is, she has begun to ask Jesus to let her see the connection between her life experience and her relationship to him, and she believes that her prayer is being answered through her insights into her defenses.

Ellen begins to see that her defenses in prayer are similar to those in her friendships. She desires close, comfortable friendships and has firm relationships, yet the kind of closeness and firmness she has with women differs from that with male friends. With women she can be close and still be self-directed, mutual, candid, and self-disclosing even about feelings of anger toward her friend. With men, she has deep doubts about whether she can be an adult and still be in relationship to them. Consequently, she defends herself against losing the old way of making the meaning of herself (i.e. as fused with a man's wishes and needs; as passively aggressive) which worked to keep men close to her, at least for a while. Her recent experience with her former lover reinforced her defenses against exposing her desire for adult intimacy. She desires an intimacy that can deal candidly and gently with conflicting desires. Because she relates to God and to Jesus as she does to the men in her life, Ellen's prayer reflects these patterns.

Eventually, Ellen begins to see that the effects of these defenses on her prayer are twofold. First, she longs for adult friendship yet finds no men who will or can respond with mutuality. She finds herself relating to Jesus and to God as Father in a similar way. She hesitates, in prayer, to speak of her deepest needs and desires, fearing that they will not be heard with interest, suspecting that they are selfish and should not be there at all. She says that she wants to do what God wants, or, more accurately, she wants to appear that way. When she is surprised by an unwanted pregnancy, she experiences very mixed emotions. On the one hand, she feels a joy that turns to apprehension when her lover refuses to bear co-responsibility for the child. On the other hand, her decision against abortion is a mixture: fear of entertaining the thought of something that "God does not want," trust that God is present in situations that are not under Ellen's control, desire to make adult decisions in this difficult matter, wondering if she can relate to God and to Jesus as an adult woman who is both angry at being pregnant in this lonely situation and is longing to go into the unknown future trusting a loving God. In other words, Ellen sees that she defends herself against the conflicts and struggles inevitably associated with real intimacy. Second, Ellen notices that when she has prayed to God as mother or related to Christ as her brother, instead of as her lover, her resistance has been lessened. When she prays with the text of Jeremiah 30:20, for example, in which God's love is modeled on Rachel's love for her children, Ellen feels freer to voice her full range of feeling, feels readier to acknowledge her true desires and her anger and frustration. In this prayer, therefore, Ellen is more open to genuine intimacy with God. When Ellen takes the advice of Teresa of Avila's autobiography (Ch. 13, #22) and looks at Christ who is looking at her, and speaks and asks, and admits her vulnerability, and delights in Jesus' accepting presence as a wise, loving friend and brother, then Ellen is much more open and less defensive about the risks that intimacy entails.

Noticing the difference between the defensiveness she feels when relating to God and Christ in the same way as she relates to the men in her life, and the greater candor and adult communication she feels when she relates to God as motherly and to Jesus as her friend and brother, helps Ellen to understand better a basic characteristic of mature spirituality. She sees what is involved in the journey from law to love. As Schneiders describes it (1986, pp. 162–167), in this journey there are risks involved in conversion from reliance on an external norm (in order to feel certain that one is doing God's will) to trust in an intimate relationship. Ellen sees that fear of autonomy and self-direction is not the same as letting go of reliance on an external norm which assures one of "being good" in God's sight. Rather, fear of self-direction can be fear of interiority, fear of the risks involved in trusting one's own religious experience. This trust is really the freedom given by God to those who have given up on the law as justification and, like the adult Jesus, give themselves over to the mercy of God who knows, and is greater than, our heart (1 Jn 3:20).

Conclusion

The final synthesis for this chapter comes through the following chart which depicts the basic correlation between spiritual direction and pastoral counseling. Their common ground is in the center and their particular characteristics are on the side labeled for each ministry.

Spiritual Direction	Common Ground	Pastoral Counseling
	1. A working alliance; goes against "defended" personality; based on drive for life and growth	
a. Source seen as indwelling Spirit of God working in and through human drive for self-transcendence (capacity to love, know, act freely)		a. Source seen as human drive for life interpreted according to various psych. theories e.g.-tend to self-actualization e.g.-reasonable ego Ult. source: God's life
b. Claim freedom yet realize our illusions and compulsions		b. Free yet restricted by lack of love, miseducation
	2. Mutual agreement or contract regarding what: a. directee/client wants b. director/counselor can do	

a.1. Facilitate RELATIONSHIP TO GOD		a.1. Help person see and solve a PROBLEM through the relationship to the counselor; faith-context appreciated
a.2. Seek and respond to God's presence with understanding and commitment; DISCERNMENT		a.2. Efficient living; mature relationships; ability to satisfy needs in love and work; various theories of maturity
b.1.a. Seek God; discernment	b.1. CLARIFY person's desire	b.1.a. Presenting problem
b.2.a. Not used to screen candidates for ordination or religious life	b.2. No conflicting loyalties	b.2.a. Not used to keep a person in a marriage or promote counselor's values
b.3. Transference NOT fostered or used	Mutual contract	b.3. Transference used; relationship to counselor as therapeutic tool

Spiritual Direction	Common Ground	Pastoral Counseling
b.4. Primary TASK: attention to God; gift of one's religious maturity as sisterly/brotherly loving support to directee and experience of how adult relationship to God progresses		b.4. Primary TASK: Use counseling skills and personal maturity to present options and support client's choice for growth
b.5. Primary ATTITUDE: active receptivity to God's movement or "agenda" in directee's life		b.5. ATTITUDE: active diagnosis, assistance, support for client's choices for growth
b.6. RELATIONSHIP: sister or brother, in Christ, to directee		b.6. RELATIONSHIP: professional counselor/therapist
b.7. TRAINING: #1 spirituality, in context of #2 psychology for religious development		b.7. TRAINING: #1 psychology/counseling skills in #2 context of theology for pastoral ministry

a.1. Share religious experience and all life as seen in this connection; seeking religious maturity which is inseparable from human maturity

a.2. Share PRAYER *development*

b.1. Feelings are indications of God's movement in one's life when seen in ENTIRE context of mature psychological life

b.8. See life-span development as opportunities for religious growth

3. PROCESS of SHARING INNER STATES: thoughts and feelings

a.1. Share struggle for human maturity (within a religious world view or faith-perspective

a.2. Sometimes pray together

b.1. Feelings and thoughts are inseparable and indicate evolution of *meaning* of self and others

Spiritual Direction	Common Ground	Pastoral Counseling
	c. Inseparable relationship between self-image and God-image; to assist one is to influence the other and raise new questions and choices	
d.1. Spiritual DARKNESS is a sign of LIFE		d.1. Psychological DEPRESSION can be *either* a sign of growth or of pathology.
	e. Darkness/depression CAN be signs of life and growth (see Chapter 6)	

	4. Defenses are seen and evaluated	
a.1. Defenses are revealed in prayer and clarified through communication about prayer	a. Religion can be used as a defense	a.1. Religion can be used as legitimation for immature human behavior
b.1. Defense is against a threatened way of making the meaning of oneself in relationship to God	b. Defend against threatened way of making meaning of oneself and others	b.1. Defend against threatened way of making meaning of self and others
c. Defend against relating to God in mutuality		
d.1. Some defending of self-image, differentiation of self from God present in even mystical prayer (e.g. Teresa of Avila).		d.1. Defense "mechanisms" can be dropped or lessened

References

Barry, William. *God and You: Prayer as Personal Relationship.* New York: Paulist, 1988.

Barry, William A. and Connolly, William J. *The Practice of Spiritual Direction.* New York: Seabury, 1982.

Brown, Raymond E. "'And the Lord Said?' Biblical Reflections on Scripture as the Word of God." *Theological Studies* 42/1 (1981), 3–19.

Capps, Donald. "Pastoral Counseling For Middle Adults: A Levinsonian Perspective." In *Clinical Handbook of Pastoral Counseling,* edited by Robert J. Wicks, Richard D. Parsons, and Donald E. Capps. New York: Paulist, 1985.

Clinebell, Howard. *Basic Types of Pastoral Counseling,* rev. ed. Nashville: Abingdon, 1984.

The Collected Works of St. Teresa of Avila. Translated by Kieran Kavanaugh, O.C.D. and Otilio Rodriguez, O.C.D. Washington, D.C.: ICS Publication, 1976+.

The Collected Works of St. John of the Cross. Translated by Kieran Kavanaugh, O.C.D. and Otilio Rodriguez, O.C.D. Washington, D.C.: ICS Publications, 1973. 2nd. ed., 1979.

Conn, Joann Wolski. "Women's Spirituality: Restriction and Reconstruction." *Cross Currents* 30/3 (Fall 1980) 293–308.

Cooke, Bernard J. "Non-Patriarchal Salvation." *Horizons* 10/1 (Spring 1983), 22–31.

Fairchild, Roy. "Guaranteed Not To Shrink: Spiritual Direction in Pastoral Care." *Pastoral Psychology* (Winter 1982), 79–95.

Gratton, Carolyn. *Trusting.* New York: Crossroad, 1982.

Merton, Thomas. *The Seven Storey Mountain.* Garden City, NY: Doubleday Image, 1970 [1948].

——— *The Sign of Jonas.* Garden City, NY: Doubleday Image, 1956 [1953].

Schneiders, Sandra M. *New Wineskins.* New York: Paulist, 1986.

——— *Spiritual Direction.* Chicago: National Sisters Vocation Conference, 1977.

The Spiritual Exercises of St. Ignatius Loyola. Translated by
Anthony Mottola. New York: Doubleday Image, 1964.

Strunk, Orlo, Jr. "A Prolegomenon to a History of Pastoral
Counseling." In *Clinical Handbook of Pastoral Counseling,*
edited by Robert J. Wicks, Richard D. Parsons, and Donald
E. Capps. New York: Paulist, 1985.

Chapter 6

Psychological Depression and Spiritual Darkness

Talk of depression and spiritual darkness raises images of sad and hopeless people, or of great saints suffering dryness in prayer, or of Jesus feeling abandoned on the cross. We admit honestly that we are afraid of these experiences and hope they never happen to us. At the same time we recognize that we all feel a bit "down" sometimes and that the well of everyone's prayer occasionally runs dry. Even this glimmer of recognition seldom leads anyone to think of depression as "normal" or to regard dryness as something to be welcomed. Nevertheless, the recognition raises questions about the inevitability of these common, painful experiences, and about the similarities and differences between depression and spiritual darkness.

This chapter focuses this search for understanding by directing these issues to the practice of pastoral counseling and spiritual direction. It demonstrates the value, in practice, of two interpretations of psychological suffering. The first theory, the meaning of spiritual darkness according to John of the Cross, can help both directors and counselors because John considers darkness within a developmental perspective. For John of the Cross, darkness is a normal, inevitable aspect of growth toward religious maturity. The second interpretation, Robert Kegan's view of depression, can assist pastoral counselors and spiritual directors because Kegan not only recognizes that depression can be severe and abnormal, but also explains how it functions as a normal aspect of development. Neither of these authors believes that psychological and spiritual darkness should be ignored or considered unimportant because they are "normal." On the contrary, they are painful experiences which call for sympathetic attention and require advice infused with knowledge and practical experience.

In order to illustrate the practical implications of these theories, I will (1) explain the meaning of spiritual darkness according to John of the Cross and describe Robert Kegan's interpretation of psychological depression; (2) demonstrate the practical implications of these theories by using them in case studies which focus either on spiritual darkness or on psychological depression; (3) explore the similarities and differences between darkness and depression.

I. Spiritual Darkness Interpreted by John of the Cross

A. *Theological Context*

1. Background. John of the Cross, a sixteenth century Spanish poet, mystic, Carmelite reformer, and scholastic theologian, conveys the meaning of spiritual darkness through two literary forms: poetry and prose. Acknowledged now as the greatest poet in the Spanish language, John communicates his own religious experience primarily in three poems, "One Dark Night," "The Spiritual Canticle," and "O Living Flame." The prose commentaries on each poem were written later and intended as advice for the people from many walks of life whom he helped in spiritual direction.

These commentaries, *The Dark Night* and *The Ascent of Mount Carmel* which interpret the first poem, and the other commentaries which bear the same names as the poetry, use scholastic theological language common to that time but difficult to understand today without modern interpretation. Fortunately, we now have excellent English translations of these works and Carmelite interpreters who show us how to gain an authentic contemporary understanding of John.[1] The following explanation relies primarily on the scholarship of Constance FitzGerald, O.C.D. (1985, 1986, 1987), who is a member of the Carmelite Forum, an association of women and men devoted to studying and teaching the writings of Carmelite theologians. John's understanding of spiritual darkness must be approached from within the wider context of his teaching about the transformation of human desire over a lifetime. Understanding the goal, pattern, and process of this transformation enables one to see how and why darkness is an inevitable part of it. If certain signs are present, darkness can be an indication of life and growth. Knowing these signs gives encouragement to those suffering in spiritual darkness, and gives support to directors and counselors who are trying to help them.

2. *The Transformation of Human Desire.* According to John of the Cross, God's action in our Christian life effects a transformation of desire over a lifetime. There is affective education by the Holy Spirit so that we can develop from a state of being unfree to a freedom whereby desire is fulfilled in the risen Christ and in his body, the Church (CWJC, 550). This transformation of desire is not a destruction of passion; rather, it is a deepening and expansion of our self so that Jesus Christ becomes the focus of our meaning.

In this transformation, grace works in and through nature so that all human energy, all power of the "harmonious" person, that is the integrated person, is spent in the love of God and love of all others in relationship to God (CWJC, 613). Here grace, which is the transforming presence of God's Spirit in us, follows a pattern that is orderly, gentle, and accommodating to the "mode of the soul." In other words, God's Spirit transforms my desire by acting through what gives meaning and love in my life, through what I cherish and what gives me support. It is, finally, a matter of leading me to deeper love not an attempt to stifle or eliminate affection or desire (CWJC, 155–156).

In *The Spiritual Canticle* John describes this transformation as a journey or search for the Beloved (God). The process involves key moments that may occur in different sequences and may be repeated many times. A central moment is the experience of self-knowledge which expands and is corrected or modified constantly in the process. Another moment is the call to self-transcendence. This is the growing urge to deepen one's love and expand the meaning of one's life. It is the "dark night" (explained in the next section) which works this out. Still another moment is the choice which enables one to have autonomy; that is, one gradually gains freedom from attachment to

self-image or to the opinion of others. Here one has the experience of one's "true self," the discovery of God within oneself.
A fifth moment might be called the "mysticism of joy in creation." The beauty and goodness of God's presence in the world
makes our desire grow. We desire this goodness and we come
up against the limits of all goodness. John maintains that we
desire God more as we experience the limits of goodness, *not*
that we desire God because we are disgusted with the world.
God's Spirit transforms our desire precisely through our relationships to people and to the world. Our sense of the limits of
goodness would not function as a purification if we did not care
about anyone or anything. Another significant moment is the
experience of darkness. Here, John insists, there can be signs
that desire is not destroyed but being transformed. Darkness
can include signs of life and growth.

B. Darkness

1. Distinguish "Darkness" from "Desolation." Since many
spiritual directors have been trained in the tradition of Ignatius
Loyola, founder of the Society of Jesus (Jesuits), it is important
to distinguish Ignatius' language of "desolation" from John's
use of "darkness." As Michael Buckley, S.J. explains (1973),
Ignatius understands desolation in contrast to consolation. The
difference between these movements of the human spirit is recognized by the ultimate direction to which the movement or
feeling leads. Consolation is that movement of the human spirit
which ultimately leads one toward God. Ordinarily movements
of joy and peace lead one to God and, therefore, are consolation. Ordinarily movements or feelings of anxiety or sadness
inhibit trust in God and, therefore, can lead one away from God
and, thus, be desolation. Restlessness or sadness, however,
could inspire one to seek deeper satisfaction in serving God
and, therefore, be consolation. In other words, desolation, for
Ignatius, is not the same as dryness in prayer or sadness or
regret; it is movement away from God. For John of the Cross,
on the other hand, negative emotions are not described as desolation; the issue is not discerning movement toward or away

from God but recognizing the present action of God revealed in the signs of life evident in the experience named by the symbol "darkness." Because this symbol is usually associated with death, John is concerned to show that in spiritual darkness quite the opposite is true. In this case, darkness is a special kind of light and life is present in a way that is not yet recognized and, therefore, could be mistaken for death.

2. *Darkness.* Although John acknowledges that darkness may be due to sin or ill health, his interest is in the darkness that accompanies growth. In his ministry of spiritual direction he is concerned for those ordinary persons who are suffering from this kind of spiritual darkness yet lack adequate advice and support. John reminds them and their spiritual directors that this darkness comes in order to allow freer, more abundant communication with God and it can be distinguished from unhealthy darkness by noting several signs (CWJC, 140–141, 313–316).

a. Signs of Life. The first sign that darkness can be an indication of spiritual growth is a breakdown of one's ordinary mode of communication with God. Love itself precipitates this darkness. Because one has grown to a certain level of communication, one can now sense its limits. A deeper communication has already begun but it is new and unfamiliar. It is, therefore, unrecognized. One judges that everything seems to be functioning in reverse. The more one tries to pray using all the methods that have ever been useful in the past, the worse things become. What helped before now hinders one's sense of communication with God.

The second sign of fruitful darkness is distaste with the things of God and with everything else. Nothing means very much any more, neither God, nor work, nor companions. One feels unable to believe in God's love, knowing that one's own mistakes have so often betrayed love. At the same time, one desires to turn to God in solitude, in prayer. One is not lax or disgusted with God. On the contrary, one desires God in the midst of this discomfort. This struggle fosters greater inner-directedness, more adult inter-dependence with God as one is gradually weaned from former supports and becomes accustomed to "so subtle a taste" of God. Taste is John's primary metaphor here.

The third and essential sign of life is one's inability to go back to one's former mode of communication with God. Still there is a "delicate" peace and nourishment that one cannot grasp. It is "like air," John says. One prefers this peace, quiet, and repose in a general loving awareness of God that lacks any particular knowledge. In other words, for some unexplainable reason, one does not want to get out of this dryness; this darkness is somehow life-giving.

John is careful to note that in order to discern whether a person's experience of darkness is an indication of spiritual growth rather than an unhealthy problem one must observe at least all three of these signs together (CWJC, 141). The first two signs—inability to pray and not caring about God or anything else—might be the result of what he calls "melancholia," meaning some physical or psychological breakdown. In modern language, these two signs might be part of a general inability to function in work and in human relationships. In this case, the suffering person is best served by turning to a physician or counselor for assistance. If a spiritual director discerns only these two signs she or he would be wise to refer the person to someone else who is trained to give full attention to these disfunctions. A spiritual director might agree to see the person at the same time as she or he is seeing a counselor, if in this way the person might discern how to respond to God in this experience of severe depression. Most of that person's energy, however, would be absorbed in the work of psychological healing. If the third sign is also present it is another matter. If the person is deeply peaceful, is maintaining work and relationships, and desires to stay with this "dry" knowledge and awareness of God that does not satisfy the senses, then the combination of these three signs indicates life and growth. Here God's Spirit is acting to transform and free the person for deeper communication.

In addition to these signs for discerning that darkness can be life-giving, John's advice includes attention to the fruits or beneficial outcomes that one should look for in the lives of persons experiencing spiritual darkness (CWJC, 314–329). First, because "God's gifts are being transferred from sense to spirit" darkness fosters inner-directedness, autonomy, a more adult responsibility for one's spiritual life. Whereas beginners in the spiritual life tend to rely heavily on the senses, that is, on the feeling of God's presence and the satisfaction of others' approval for their motivation and support, those whose love has developed further now realize the limits of this kind of love and, in dryness or darkness, become less sensual (in this sense) and more spiritual, in the sense of being more inner-directed. A second fruit is energy. John stresses that spiritual darkness does not incapacitate a person; on the contrary, he or she has strength and energy to work. In life-giving darkness one is somehow empowered. Another benefit, and a recurring theme in John's explanation, is "peace." There is deep peace in which one has a dark yet habitual remembrance of God and a desire not to turn back on one's spiritual road. One of the greatest benefits of living in spiritual darkness is self-knowledge. Like his friend, Teresa of Avila, John speaks constantly about self-knowledge as the "nourishment" of the person growing in spiritual maturity. Lastly, one experiences greater integration in life. John expresses this as growth in the "practice of virtue." Because he understands virtue in the same way as Thomas Aquinas, John means that a person who is virtuous, who is acting in faith, hope, charity, prudence, and so forth, is bringing all his or her natural powers of intellect and will to their highest peak of efficiency. In contemporary language, the person is becoming more integrated.

b. Practical Advice. John includes five points of practical advice in his suggestions for persons living in spiritual darkness and for their spiritual directors. First and foremost, be patient and trust that God has not abandoned you. Second, "rest" in prayer and in God even though you seem to "waste time." In other words, stay with the experience; admit and acknowledge the darkness and do not worry that your prayer is not producing any good thoughts or feelings or resolutions as it might have

in the past. Third, be "free." Do not hesitate to be free of the
fatigue of analysis that sometimes accompanies meditation. Be
free of the need to be "accomplishing something" in prayer or
in your spiritual life. Fourth, be "attentive." Cooperate with
the third sign of healthy darkness mentioned above; that is,
continue to be attentive to God without an effort or desire to
taste or feel God in the way you did before. Be attentive to God
"without comfort, security, or dependency." Fifth, be aware of
the fact that for some people this darkness "comes and goes."
We cannot, John says, "be weaned all at once." The metaphor
of weaning indicates that this is an experience of growing maturity, therefore it is normal. Its connection with mothering
reminds us of God's care and fidelity.

All of the explanation above is part of John's teaching about
the "night of the senses," which is one of two types of darkness.
The other, the "night of the spirit," is a darkness that is felt
even more deeply in the entire person. In this night the issue
is not so much comfort as whatever has given assurance and
meaning before. Here, John warns, there is no experience of
support and one is completely vulnerable. In the person's spirit
there is complete loss of meaning; one's memory of all that once
gave meaning now results in a feeling of being "mocked" by
the past; the "abandoned heart" seems all alone. John stresses
that a person never chooses this dark path which can bring one
to the abyss of atheism. God calls some into this darkness of
contemplation so that "complete divinization" can transform
the person into one who "loves with God's own love." Thérèse
of Lisieux (1873–1897), a French Carmelite, experienced this
deepest darkness for eighteen months and described it in her
memoirs, *Story of a Soul* (1975).

Kieran Kavanaugh O.C.D., translator of John of the Cross,
notes (1987, p. 179): because of the interdependence of sense
and spirit, the one purification cannot be present without the
other. John describes the first night, which is common, as characteristic of beginners passing into the stage of "proficients";
the second, which is rare, is that of "proficients" as they pass
into the stage of the "perfect." This spiritual developmental

perspective will be correlated with Robert Kegan's psychological view in Section III which compares and contrasts darkness and depression.

C. Practical Implications: A Case Study

1. Value for Today. Although written in the sixteenth century, John's advice about responding to spiritual darkness can reach the hearts and minds of persons today. First, because it is not abstract theological speculation but expression of John's own Christian experience examined over a lifetime, its power is that of experience speaking to experience. It awakens persons to their own experience of God. Second, because it interprets and evaluates experience according to the teaching of scripture, John's advice has the authentic ring of the familiar pattern of God's action in the life of Israel's prophets and in Jesus. Third, John's advice has the persuasive power of years of practical experience in the ministry of spiritual direction. His suggestions have been refined through many conversations with those who suffered the darkness and demonstrated the growth that he describes.

We will see in the case study below the advantages given to both partners in spiritual direction when they follow John's advice regarding spiritual darkness. (This case, like the others I created for this book, is fictitious yet inspired by many years in the ministry of spiritual direction.) Instead of being overwhelmed by problems or baffled by mystery, both persons can become partners in redemptive action that is directed by God's Spirit.

2. Description of Annmarie's Darkness. Annmarie asks for companionship in spiritual direction because she feels sad, confused, and tired. Annmarie is thirty-five years old, a member of a religious congregation for fifteen years, a theology teacher devoted to high school students, a person entrusted with administrative positions in her community. She approaches Janice because Janice, although not a sister, has a reputation for understanding and appreciating sisters, and for believing that feminism is compatible with the tradition of Christian spirituality.

Annmarie begins by describing the way she has been feeling and thinking for the past ten months. "My religious life seems to be falling apart. I'm not sure if I can remain a sister feeling so 'phony,' so unable to minister to anyone else's faith when my own isn't there anymore. I can't seem to pray. I feel closer to a woman, a fellow-teacher, who isn't a sister than I do to most of the sisters in my community. This friend shares my interest in feminism but isn't interested in religion or theology. She has really opened my eyes through a lot of books we have read and discussed together. Now that I have absorbed these feminist ideas I see the church's neglect and abuse of women and I can't relate to Christ anymore. I wish I could pray but I can't and I don't know where to turn. Sometimes at the eucharist I cry because it used to mean so much to me; but now I just feel alienated or sort of 'dead' when I hear all this masculine language for God and see only male clergy who don't seem to realize how bad things are. Some days I just feel overwhelmed, helpless and tired.' "

Janice, guided primarily by the classical teaching of John of the Cross but also by Kegan's model of an evolving self, gently responds to Annmarie. Janice is peacefully alert and confident because she has reliable guidelines for recognizing the outline of God's action here. Janice responds first in a general way by reflecting back to Annmarie that she hears her exhaustion and confusion and she appreciates this chance to contemplate God's presence in Annmarie's life. In this way Janice begins to join Annmarie in her painful experience and communicate to her a conviction that God is surely present in what feels to Annmarie like the absence of God. Then Janice becomes more specific.

Janice next wants to test the adequacy of her own grasp of Annmarie's experience and communicate to Annmarie that she is understood. At the same time, Janice wants to test her intuition that Annmarie is actually describing, in her own way, the signs that John of the Cross presents as indications of spiritual growth, not of the death that Annmarie fears.

Janice: Am I expressing your experience accurately if I say that you feel that you can't pray now in any of the ways that you used to follow?

Annmarie: Right, nothing works. The more I try, the worse it gets.

Janice: I felt sad when you said that you cried at the eucharist because it used to mean so much to you and now it's just painful or alienating. You seem to regret how you feel and wish it were some other way.

Annmarie: I feel so terrible. I'm sad, and I'm mad, and I just wish I knew what to do.

Janice (asks her most important question): What do you most want to do, Annmarie?

Annmarie (her voice choking with emotion): I want to know how, or if, I can still relate to Christ.

Annmarie confirms Janice's intuition and gives her a clue about which aspect of Annmarie's experience Janice can now suggest that they focus upon. Janice now recognizes the signs that this spiritual darkness is life-giving; with Annmarie's cooperation, it can be the Spirit's education of human desire to allow deeper communication and more inclusive love. Annmarie demonstrates an inability to communicate with God in the former ways that gave meaning and satisfaction: John's first sign. Second, Annmarie has distaste for the eucharist, and her work gives little satisfaction. Most important, the third sign accompanies the other two: Annmarie desires to be attentive to God in the midst of this dryness and pain. She expresses this as a longing to find a way to reconcile her feminist questions (e.g. Is patriarchal religion intrinsically sexist? Can a male savior save women?) with her dedication to Christ. Her desire for spiritual direction also demonstrates the third sign: willingness to stay with this darkness, to search for Christ in this "desert," to look long and hard at this experience in a way that would keep her attentive to God, to do the work of discerning the appropriate response to this hidden presence of God.

Annmarie's focus on Christ and on feminism suggests to Janice the way she can begin to support Annmarie's discernment. It also seems to be the only aspect of Annmarie's pain that might be lessened. The suffering that characterizes the first two signs, namely the broken communication and distaste for life, cannot be alleviated precisely because it is the pain that accompanies the loss of a less mature love. To alleviate it would be to regress, to refuse deeper life. Annmarie's struggle to remain attentive to Christ's hidden presence might be helped by encouragement to freedom. Janice suggests both a freedom to explore a new feminist perspective on the New Testament witness to Christ and freedom to pray without analyzing her darkness. Realizing that Annmarie's pain involves a loss of meaning, Janice asks her if she thinks reading might help. When Annmarie expresses great interest, Janice invites her to reflect and pray with Sandra Schneiders' study, *Women and the Word* (1986), which responds directly to some of the issues implicit in Annmarie's anguish about Christ and feminism. Regarding freedom in prayer, Janice invites Annmarie to refrain from worrying that time given to prayer should "accomplish something" to resolve her anguish. Janice encourages her to feel free to stop using images or words in prayer, when these no longer help her to be in touch with God, and instead simply be aware of her longing for Christ, since this desire itself is a revelation of Christ's longing for her. Janice reminds her of John's advice for someone in this situation: ". . . going to prayer means remaining in ease and freedom of spirit" (CWJC, 318). Lastly, Janice invites her to share her experience of this kind of prayer when they meet again.

Having examined the initial spiritual-direction phase which focused on discernment of the signs that Annmarie's darkness was life-giving, let us move ahead in Annmarie's life. A brief look at the following year of her life shows the "fruits" or beneficial outcomes which Annmarie subsequently experienced in this darkness and includes examples of the practical advice that guided Janice in her companionship with Annmarie.

3. Benefits of This Darkness. During the following year of spiritual direction Annmarie experienced the fruit of the Spirit's transformation of her love in darkness. While she was already a mature adult, she became even more inner-directed

and less concerned with others' approval for motivation and
support. For example, she persevered in finding a combination
of ministries that suited her talents more than the institutional
needs of her community. Although tired, naturally, from her
struggles with letting go of her former "idols" of God and of a
"good sister," Annmarie was not incapacitated. On the contrary, she sustained her devotion to community life, insisting,
for example, that she was unwilling to live with her sisters on a
superficial level and was willing to share her vulnerabilities,
believing that they also needed to share theirs. In addition,
Annmarie experienced a new kind of peace. This was not an
absence of conflict within her nor an elimination of struggles to
live her feminist spirituality within a patriarchal church. For
her, the peace centered on a new experience of the meaning of
"charity." She was discovering, from experience, that what she
used to think meant "being nice to everyone, silently tolerating
community dissension," now meant "giving the time to
develop the level of sharing that intimacy demands." This experience gave her a deep, "dry" satisfaction, not an emotional
"high." She believed that she was now beginning to experience
the true "shalom" of the gospel. All of the above became
aspects of another fruit: self-knowledge as "nourishment." A
theme in her spiritual direction conversations became, "I can't
believe how much better I understand myself these days. Over
and over I see that my loving people no longer means that I
have the 'power' to change them. Maybe it's just that I'm getting older and getting over the enthusiasm of my energetic
twenties." When Annmarie would raise this issue of the connection between psychological and spiritual growth, Janice
would encourage her to reflect on this issue and sometimes
explicitly refer to John of the Cross' teaching about God's Spirit
always working *through* what we know and care about in our
ordinary lives. If the Spirit worked through something else it
would not have any effect on us. It could not function as "purification" if it was not deeply embedded in our ordinary psychology, our minds and hearts. This correlation of nature and
grace in the development of self-knowledge and spiritual maturity is also an example of the last fruit of darkness that John

mentions: integration. For Annmarie, the integration slowly emerged in a conviction that her life in a community of sisters was beginning to "make more sense to me." She was struggling and learning how to incorporate friends who were not sisters into her life in community. This friendship with non-sisters had been discouraged during her earlier religious life so that she had tended to suspect that caring about these friends was "dividing" her attention from her primary commitment. Now she realized that authentic religious life aims to make a person more inclusive, not more separated from those who have not chosen consecrated celibacy. Annmarie also felt that her honesty about her struggles with sexist liturgy and her candor about her discomfort with community prayer had led others to share their struggles with faith and thus led to more honest faith-sharing and a more integrated connection between life and prayer.

Janice, using Kegan's developmental perspective, noticed how Annmarie's spiritual development correlated with Kegan's description of the evolving self-directed person. For example, Annmarie experienced the limits of control in relationships and she gained new insight into the personal demands of authentic intimacy. These correlations will be examined further in the last part of this chapter.

4. Advice for the Director. All the benefits of Annmarie's experience of darkness developed while Janice followed John of the Cross' five practical directives intended for both director and directee. Janice used them as a kind of "voice of greater experience" assuring her of a tried-and-true procedure to follow in this ambiguous experience of supporting Annmarie in her darkness. When Annmarie's own questions or struggles directly related to any of these procedures, Janice would reassure her sometimes by explicitly referring to John's teaching. In other words, Janice had so personally appropriated these suggestions that they became a natural part of the way she discerned, for herself, the appropriate response to God's presence in Annmarie's life and in her own life as Annmarie's sister in Christ and spiritual friend. Patience and trust were the most basic response. Janice's contemplative attention in the spiritual direction conversations was centered in trust that the Spirit was always guiding Annmarie "in silence and in darkness" and was supporting Janice as she asked Annmarie to consider various issues.

According to John's second admonition, Janice encouraged Annmarie to "rest" in this experience of God even though she might feel that she was "wasting time"; that is, she encouraged Annmarie to stay with this experience of darkness, to stay especially with whatever was her present experience of prayer and try to express during their spiritual direction conversations whatever she had felt or thought in prayer. Janice advised Annmarie not to worry about anything that did or, more accurately, did not happen in prayer or in life. It is better, Janice emphasized, simply to rest peacefully with the experience, whatever it involves, even if that includes feelings of anger or fear of abandonment. "Rest," in this case, can imply peaceful courage to look honestly at whatever emerges in prayer and in the whole of one's life and not monitor or worry that "I should not feel this way."

John's third point of practical advice makes this meaning of "rest" even more explicit. He says, "be free." Janice therefore encouraged Annmarie to feel free to explore all the feminist theology that appealed to her, free to admit that her faith did not give her much meaning now, free to admit that "I don't know where I'm going, but I know I can't go back to the way I used to pray and think and be," free to let go of trying to "accomplish something" by having her spiritual life be completely consistent and controlled.

John's next piece of advice became more and more significant. "Be attentive to God," John says, "without comfort, security, or dependency." As Annmarie lost her former way of understanding prayer and religious life she felt "phony" in her ministry of religious education, and hesitant about taking her turn at designing evening prayer for her sisters; she felt guilty and superficial at times. This is when she most needed John's advice about resting attentively in God without security or dependency. That is, Annmarie needed to trust in God's love and let go of the security of relying on her own "good works" or "virtue" in order to "earn" God's love and thus feel secure in prayer. Here the example of another Carmelite saint was a powerful reminder. Annmarie was encouraged by the fact that the holier Thérèse of Lisieux became, the less surprised she was that she was full of faults; moreover, the deeper Thérèse was plunged into a darkness of faith the more she willingly identified with agnostics and sinners and, at the same time, peacefully trusted in God's loving mercy.

Annmarie's darkness continues, yet she would not want her life to be any other way. She has gained dark knowledge of what John means by saying that God "weans" us. She experiences God's maternal care of her, not as a child who cannot be entrusted with the complex truth of life, but as an adult daughter who is, like the disciples in Mark's gospel, entrusted with the ministry even as she experiences her own need to grow into deeper faith. Janice continues to praise God for this gift of contemplating God's work in Annmarie's life and for the gift of the practical advice in John of the Cross' teaching about spiritual darkness.

Although Annmarie demonstrates some symptoms of depression—sadness, fatigue, loss of meaning—her experience is more accurately described as spiritual darkness. Again, although she is helped by some methods of pastoral counseling for depressed persons—patient attention to her feelings of confusion and threat, relativizing relationships that had been ultimate—her development is best served by spiritual direction. The relationship between these two experiences will become clearer after we examine Kegan's view of depression.

II. Psychological Depression According to Robert Kegan

A. General Background

Kegan (1982) would agree with other theorists that depression is manifested by certain characteristic behavior.[2] Depressed persons are unhappy or dejected. Their appetite and sleep are disturbed. Movement is often slow and fatigued.

There is loss of interest in work, family, life in general. One's energy level is low. One feels worthless or guilty. It is difficult to think, and thoughts that do arise are sometimes of death and even of suicide.

Kegan also agrees with the judgment that depression can be more or less severe, and that some severe depression can be helped through medication. Those with severe depression lose contact with reality and manifest more of the symptoms mentioned above. These severely ill persons require long-term care and the attention of highly trained therapists. These cases are beyond the scope of this book which is directed to counselors and directors who feel equipped to help those whose depression is less severe and who, therefore, manifest milder forms of these symptoms. This milder depression is often precipitated by the normal difficulties of life such as the death of a spouse or the loss of a friend or a job. Kegan calls this less severe depression "normal" and the more severe depression "abnormal." His understanding of the cause for depression explains why he considers some depression to be normal.

Before explaining Kegan's answer to the question of why people become depressed, we will note several other answers to this question, as summarized in Bootzin's and Acocella's *Abnormal Psychology* (1984), and then see how Kegan's position includes some of these other insights. The psychodynamic theory of depression maintains that depression is a massive defense of the ego or self when a person cannot cope with life. Depression is understood here to be anger turned inward. For example, a depressed person may be unconsciously angry at a loved one whose death left him feeling alone and helpless. Therapy within the psychodynamic perspective would focus on gaining an awareness of this anger and being able to express it outwardly rather than turn the anger inward. Object-relations theory, a development within psychodynamic psychology, links depression with the loss of an object (i.e. person) that gave affirmation, love, and identity. Therapy, within this framework, concentrates on recovering, or making available, an empathic person who can function as psychological "oxygen" for the depressed person whose life-breath has been lost. Existential psychology holds that depression is caused by a failure to live authentically. It is a failure to make choices according to one's own values, a failure to be self-directed. Existential therapy would focus on confronting one's own values and goals and act ing on them. Cognitive psychology, especially that of Aaron Beck, maintains that self-defeating thoughts are the primary cause of depression. Because thoughts that breed hopelessness are believed to be the cause of the emotional condition that is depression, this type of therapy focuses on cognitive retraining. For example, cognitive therapy works to remove self-defeating thoughts and replace them with thoughts that picture the self as "a winner" rather than "a loser."

Kegan's understanding of depression is part of his wider constructive-developmental perspective explained in previous chapters, and incorporates insights from all the major theories of depression. For Kegan, depression involves the loss of self (as in ego psychology), loss of an object (as in object relations theory), and loss of meaning (as in existential psychology and cognitive psychology). The following explanation of these themes will focus on Kegan's most significant contribution to our understanding of depression: how and why it occurs at different phases of life-span development.

B. Depression

1. Definition and Description. Depression is a variation on the theme of affective-cognitive finding and losing. Recall, from Chapter 3, that from Kegan's perspective the ground of affectivity-cognition is the evolution from being undifferentiated from others to being more differentiated or distinct from others. This movement occurs precisely so that one might be really related to others and not be simply fused with them. This evolution of personal life is a constant renegotiation of the balance of what self means and what the object (e.g. another person) means. The source of e-motion, as Kegan puts it, is the motion of meaning whereby I defend, surrender, and reconstruct a center; that is, I construct a type of balance or negotiation of the meaning of myself and what is other. For example, a child's "separation anxiety," in this perspective, is not the loss of an object (e.g. the mother) because she does not yet wholly exist as a differentiated person who could be lost. Rather, this anxiety is the loss of what is becoming "the old me" (i.e. "me" as fused-with-my-mother), the loss of the self from which I am not yet sufficiently differentiated so as to feel comfortable. I (the anxious child) am anxious because I am not yet able to integrate that lost part of myself as "other."

From Kegan's constructive-developmental perspective (1982, pp. 81–85, 129–32, 185–86), the anger and loss which are common features of depression in most theories are viewed as developmental phases within depression itself. Notice how this works in the case of the depression commonly experienced by a young person going away to a residential college. Such a young woman or man is usually embedded in the interpersonal relationships of friends and family. For example, recall the case of Lambert (Chapter 3) who, in his first semester in college, feels loss and anger as aspects of his depression. The loss is a first phase. An affective experience of loss or differentiation of his "old self" makes Lambert feel anxious and depressed. The normal processes of life which generated a beginning of the integration of *having* a relationship to his family rather than primarily *being* a part of his family made him feel angry. He expressed this anger as a feeling directed at his family because they would not agree to have him return home. From Kegan's perspective this anger is best understood not as anger at his parents but as a repudiation of the "me-that's-not-me," as anger at Lambert's "old-me," an anger that defends him from going back to the old balance of independence and attachment (in this case, fusion) which is Lambert's "old me." The anger allows him to begin to learn how to be at home in the world of a new reorganization of his self-other coherence which can take account of the complexity of relationship and separation now facing the "me-that-is-becoming."

What is a normal loss for a young college student could become an abnormal loss or severe depression if the person's "culture of embeddedness," that is his close friends or family, leave him through desertion, death, or divorce just when his normal independence is taking place. This abandonment prevents him from being able to reintegrate these persons from the vantage point of his new "self." The severe depression can be a repudiation of the self he is becoming and be brought on because he has no support for resolving the question or threat he experiences.

Both severe and normal depression are based on one's anxiety at having one's balance (of self-object) either threatened or questioned. Experiencing depression as a "threat-to" one's balance (of self-object) occurs when one feels that "I" am secure in the meaning of myself, but my "world" is doubtful, strange, or alien. I doubt that I can cope in the world as it has become and thus feel threatened by the world. Experiencing depression as a "question" of my balance (of self-object) occurs when I am not clear about either the meaning of my "self" or my "world" and, therefore, experience deep tension.

2. *Different Types of Depression at Different Phases of Development.* A normal depression can be expected, according to Kegan (1982, pp. 268–273), when a person evolves out of one phase of development into another. Evolving out of each phase, one feels an assault on the current balance (of self-other). At each phase there is a particular concern that is experienced as either a "threat-to" that balance or a "question" of that balance. Continuing this book's focus on adults, we will examine the concern, threat, and question that are characteristic of depression in two phases of adult development: phase three (self-other are embedded in the interpersonal), and phase four (self-other are embedded in control of relationships, work, and so forth).

Evolution out of embeddedness in the interpersonal is often accompanied by the following type of depression. One's central *concern* is an assault on the interpersonal balance of constructing the meaning of "self" and "other." If I experience the assault as a *threat-to* this balance, my self is felt to be secure while my world is doubtful. For example, if I am a young adult whose parent or girlfriend dies or leaves me I may not doubt my identity but my balance is threatened because I doubt that I can cope with the new way my world has become. I therefore feel unbearably lonely, deserted, betrayed by friends and family, stained by these feelings, by this world. If I experience this assault in a different way, as a radical *question*, then neither my self nor my world is clear or comfortable. For example, if I am a mother who is fused with her husband and children, when I return to college or begin a career I can begin to feel depressed. I feel deep tension because I feel simultaneously vulnerable to fusing, to loss of my self as my own person, *and* I feel selfish or heartless as a result of considering "myself first" in my concern to be more independent, more differentiated from the others in whom I have been fused.

Evolution from embeddedness in control is accompanied by depression that can be described another way. Here one's central concern is with assault on the control aspects of work and relationships. For example, if I am a husband who learns that my wife plans to divorce me, or if I am the only woman in a law firm and learn that I have been refused a partnership I experience this assault as a *threat-to* my balance (of self-other). I feel that I know who I am while my world has become so strange that I doubt that I can cope in this new world. I therefore feel humiliated, empty, out of control, compromised. If I experience this assault in a different way, as a *question*, it becomes a situation in which neither my self nor my world is clear. Here I experience deep tension because, at the same time, I feel vulnerable to crippling self-attack, to identifying with my performance, to isolation in self-containment, unable to be close to another *and* I feel weak, ineffective, out of control; indeed, I can feel evil (because uncontrolled), decadent, without identity in my society or my religion or my family.

Case Studies. In order to illustrate Kegan's general suggestions for a therapeutic response to depression, we will look at cases of women and men whose depression is experienced as an assault either on the interpersonal balance or on the institutional balance. My experience confirms Kegan's judgment that more women than men become fixed in their development at the interpersonal balance, so the first and most detailed case will be that of a younger woman and the second case will be one of an older woman with some of the same symptoms of depression. Men tend to manifest this type of depression when they are young. For an example of this refer back to the story of Lambert in Chapter 3. Depression experienced as an assault on the institutional balance will be exemplified in the case of a man and a woman who are feminists. How feminism figures in their depression will be evident in the examples.

a. *Assault on the Interpersonal Balance: Maureen (young adult).* Maureen is a twenty-five year old graduate student in divinity school who is intelligent, articulate, and popular. When her grades dropped, her class participation became minimal, and her appearance was consistently sad, her professor recognized symptoms of depression and suggested that she talk to Polly, a psychologist in the pastoral counseling services. Maureen told Polly how tired and confused she felt. She used to be so enthusiastic about ministry, so capable of writing and discussing, but now she can't seem to get involved. Polly listened carefully and eventually communicated to Maureen that she understood Maureen's experience *as Maureen experienced it:* thoughts and feelings of loneliness, betrayal, and disillusionment. During her first year in graduate school Maureen fell in love with Jack, a divinity student who shared her interests. Although they both had to devote a great deal of time to study, they managed to spend many evenings and weekends together. In the following year Maureen felt things changing dramatically. While her plans for ordination and ministry demanded travel in the next few years to wherever she could find a challenging job, Jack's plans to obtain a doctorate would keep him at the university for those years. Whereas she was interested in a long-term relationship and willing to struggle with the difficulties that might entail, Jack was frank about his inability and unwillingness to plan for the future. Yet Jack maintained that he loved Maureen. Although Maureen told Polly that she felt secure in her sense of herself as directed toward a career in ministry, she was equally firm in her desire for a permanent relationship with Jack. She now felt lonely and unable to "reach" Jack. She felt disillusioned and betrayed by those who led her to believe that career and marriage could go together. She felt confused and unable to cope with her world of graduate studies and job applications. She felt tired, "blocked" in her writing, confused in the face of daily demands, unable to figure out why she could not "get going" with her life, angry with herself for feeling so "immature," yet unable to "snap out of it."

Polly recognizes the signs of a person whose depression is experienced as an assault on the evolutionary balance in which one creates the meaning of herself and others primarily in terms of relationship. The two basic human longings for self-direction and for connection are, in Maureen, balanced primarily in the "direction" of herself as "being" Jack's lover and friend rather than "having" this relationship. She demonstrates that the evolutionary balance is beginning to shift toward more self-direction, yet this new "self-directed me" is not yet well accepted and integrated. Maureen is only now beginning to know, that is, experience, the "price" of her new growth. She is now beginning to experience that one longing (i.e. for self-direction) comes at the price of feeling less "support," that is, less identity or less collapsed psychic space, in the interpersonal. Like most women, Maureen values relationships *and* differentiation, and wants "differentiation *in* relationship," as Jean Baker Miller describes women's psychology (1976, 1987). The problem here, however, and the root of her depression is Maureen's over-identification with a relationship combined with insufficient social situations which reward her for taking responsibility for her own preferences and career initiatives. Maureen experiences a "threat-to" this interpersonal balance when Jack, for his part, demonstrates an identity that does not include a long-term relationship to Maureen and focuses his conversation with her on his own need to be "honest" about his future plans and gives little or no attention to what would be a naturally therapeutic environment for her.

Polly's response to Maureen's experience of depression will center on three goals which will create a naturally therapeutic environment. First, Polly will help Maureen *stay with the experience* of loss, isolation, and coldness that she feels when she is not fused with the interpersonal, in this case, with Jack. Polly helps Maureen stay with the experience in two ways. (1) Polly communicates to Maureen that she grasps Maureen's experience in the way that Maureen experiences; thus Maureen can relax her attention away from trying to hold her uncertain world together because she now senses that Polly is there in that uncertain world with her; indeed, she can begin to be aware instead of what (balance) she is defending and why she defends it. (2) Polly stays with Maureen not by giving advice but by surfacing the degree to which Maureen is willing to do the "work" that growth into *differentiation* in relationship requires.

Polly's second goal is to help Maureen *stay with the new self-knowledge* that emerges when Maureen looks carefully at her experience of loneliness and betrayal. Staying with loneliness gradually reveals to Maureen a loss of a "me-that's-no longer-me," the loss of a me that enjoyed life and work and study because "I" *was* a relationship (to Jack). Maureen knows this "old" me is lost for two reasons; she lost her former enjoyment of life and studies, and she lost her ability to feel she could cope with studies. She also begins to know she feels angry at herself for being so "immature," and angry at Jack for being unwilling to negotiate any of his plans. Her new self-knowledge includes also the realization that, in spite of her deep discomfort, she has not withdrawn from school. She also feels some security and certitude. She is sure that she loves Jack and that love is worth the suffering it entails. She is also sure that she wants a career in ministry. Maureen puts a high priority on all friendship and ranks love on the same level of value as success in her career. Staying with this new self-knowledge gradually enables Maureen to see that her choice to stay in school despite the discomfort and difficulty reveals a "new me," a self that is tipping the balance of attachment-independence in the direction of greater self-direction. Maureen will be more likely to stay with her new self-knowledge if Polly helps her understand why perseverance will not remove conflict; rather, this new self-knowledge brings the conflict inside because one now has greater "interiority," and, therefore, more awareness and the possibility of more pain. Conflict, however, is a normal component of every meeting of different personalities, so the only appropriate response is to feel the freedom to expect and explore conflict and find creative ways to deal with it.

Maureen's awareness of her choice to be self-directed allows her to consider a goal that Polly realized from the beginning would be central to Maureen's development. Polly's experience with Maureen's type of depression led Polly to judge that Maureen's "evolving self" would call her to relativize her relationship to Jack. Greater maturity, that is, ability to deal with the more complex relationship to Jack and to her career that now faces Maureen, calls her to bring the organization of the meaning of her self and others into a new coherence that can take account of this complexity. This new coherence involves relativizing the relationship that had been ultimate. Maureen must decide to do the work of *having* a relationship to Jack rather than *being* a relationship. Her decision to stay in school despite the discomfort and her decision to seek counseling reveal that she is willing to consider this ultimate relationship within some wider context. Actually relativizing the relationship will be supported in counseling sessions through attention to meaning. Because Maureen's depression is rooted in the loss of an old meaning of her "self" and "other," growth out of the depression will be helped by Polly doing three things: (1) refusing to ally herself with Maureen's "old meaning of me" (fusion with an other) that is now threatened and defended, (2) supporting the "emerging meaning of me" (self-directed) that is uncertain and in need of education to new meaning, (3) staying with Maureen in her defensive struggle in order to be reintegrated into the more mature, more complex relationships now facing Maureen.

Because, in Kegan's perspective, the focus of counseling is the evolution of *meaning*, the process could include methods typical of cognitive therapy such as monitoring of self-defeating thoughts (e.g. "Life is worthless without Jack"), and reeducation of beliefs. Polly could draw out Maureen's beliefs about these issues: for example, does "Life is worthless without Jack" mean the same as "Life is worthless without love and friendship"? Which is truer and why? Maureen would then explore ways in which she could make choices to develop or sustain the truth in her life.

In what ways is this case an example of pastoral counseling? Polly's own faith, and welcoming of Maureen as her sister in Christ, and her concern to focus on the Christian values of love and responsibility for one's vocation make Polly's counseling pastoral from the perspective of the one doing the counseling. It is also pastoral in so far as the content is Christian without being explicitly about religious faith. However, Polly might well hear Maureen refer to her Christian education as one reason why she has such strong convictions about the primacy of love and friendship over any other value. Then the content would obviously become explicitly pastoral. If clarification of Christian conviction becomes an explicit goal of the counseling relationship, that would highlight the goal Polly always has in her ministry: welcome her clients into the full humanity which God desires for every person; promote that maturity which evolves beyond autonomy into mutuality and the authentic intimacy which reveals God's own love.

b. Assault on the Interpersonal Balance: Irene (middle age). Irene experiences the assault on the interpersonal balance much later in life than Maureen. Irene is fifty-two, the mother of two sons and a daughter who are now living at a distance from Irene and her husband Joe. Irene's lack of interest in eating or going anywhere, her expressions of envy and constant complaints about Joe's involvement in business prompt Joe to insist that Irene talk to their pastor about her problems.

Pastor Walsh recognizes the root of Irene's depression as an experience of assault on her way of making the meaning of herself and others. She has created the meaning of herself as *being* part of four relationships: she *is* mother to three children and wife to Joe. Their absence makes her feel threatened because she doubts that she can cope with the world as it has become without these people functioning as the reason for her "getting up in the morning."

Irene and Pastor Walsh begin a companionship in conversation in which Walsh unconditionally accepts Irene and, at the same time, presents Irene with the opportunity to move from a less mature to a more mature way of making the meaning of herself and others. Walsh reaches out to Irene, moves into her horizon of the questions and answers she can now give about the meaning of her life, and awaits her choice to do the work that growth demands. Responding to her dependent depression, Walsh presents Irene with opportunities for growth by confirming, contradicting and continuing with her in ways that suit her particular evolving balance of differentiation in relationship. He therefore confirms her capacity for self-sacrifice in relationships; yet he contradicts her embeddedness in relationships by refusing her attempts to be fused with him and by insisting that she assume responsibility for her own preferences and choices; he also faithfully continues to companion her as she struggles, defends, argues, chooses to take responsibility for her initiatives; all the while he agrees that society and the church have rewarded women for immature fusion with relationships and that the church, especially, ignored women's need for independence. Walsh's fidelity to Irene in her struggles enables her, eventually, to integrate their relationship into a richer, more complex network of relationships to Joe, her children, and her new, mid-life career in teaching.

 c. Assault on the Institutional Balance: Al and Barbara. Al and Barbara are in their early forties, are successful sales representatives for competing companies, consider themselves feminists, and are each divorced after marrying someone whom they met in college. They meet, begin to fall in love, then experience extreme anxiety and frustration in their relationship. Both experience mild depression that is manifest in unusual fatigue, falling sales, and isolation from their colleagues. Both Al and Barbara agree to counseling, at the urging of friends. Their counselor, Marvin, has recently revised his counseling perspective using insights from feminist psychology and recognizes their depression as a "self-evaluative" depression rooted in their experience of assault on the institutional balance.

 Al and Barbara have the same type of depression yet experience it in different ways. Al feels secure in the meaning of himself as a person in control, as a self-directed, autonomous person, but is threatened by Barbara's demands for psychological intimacy. He is a feminist; therefore he assumes women will have careers and is not threatened by her independence. Nevertheless, his experience with independent women has never before led to the deep attraction which he now feels toward Barbara; and his experience with dependent women, such as his former wife, has been sexual but not really intimate. That is, there has been no demand for mutuality and no acceptance of mutual psychological vulnerability as valuable or appropriate. Al's experience of depression, therefore, is one of feeling threatened because he doubts that he can cope with the world as it has become: one of relationship with this woman who refuses to settle for superficial sharing of themselves. Barbara, on the other hand, experiences depression as profound questioning of her way of making the meaning of herself and others. She feels deep tension between isolation in self-containment in order to maintain control of the life she worked so hard to attain after her divorce, and feeling out of control, feeling swallowed up as a result of not being "altogether" when she risks sharing her vulnerability and values psychological intimacy. Barbara's feminism enables her to value both control and the vulnerability needed for intimacy. Her long years embedded in relationships were detrimental for her growth yet they had a positive "residue" also. This gave her experience of the value of vulnerability for attaining authentic intimacy. Al's past experience of spending only a short time embedded in relationships (as a high school student) makes it now more difficult for him to evolve out of embeddedness in control.

For both Al and Barbara, the counseling process will confirm the same capacities: their independence and capacity for self-definition. For Barbara, however, it will also confirm her capacity for intimate, non-mediated relationships. Toward Al, Marvin will respond differently on this same issue. Here Marvin will contradict Al's flight from this capacity by not accepting a mediated, intellectualized, non-intimate relationship with him. In this way Marvin presents Al with the opportunity to choose the work involved in growth toward more mature relationships with him and with Barbara. Toward Barbara, Marvin will contradict her occasional moves to retreat from insisting on psychological intimacy with Al. With both Al and Barbara, Marvin will be a faithful companion so that they may, eventually, integrate him and each other into a richer, more complex set of loving relationships.

In the cases of Maureen, Irene, Lambert (in Chapter 3), Al, and Barbara, depression is experienced as a variation on themes of loss, anger, threat, and questioning. The assault on a particular developmental balance (of differentiation-in-relationship) is experienced as a particular type of threat or question. The counselor responds to each person by confirming, contradicting, and continuing according to the needs of each balance.

This treatment of depression has repeated themes noted in the earlier study of spiritual darkness. Both are experiences of loss, threat, questioning, new self-knowledge, freedom, and intimacy. Having examined each experience in detail, we can now clarify their similarities and differences.

III. Depression and Darkness:
Comparison and Contrast

There are several practical reasons for clarifying the similarities and differences between depression and spiritual darkness. (1) So that counselors and directors do not mistake one for the other and, consequently, prevent suffering persons from receiving the kind of assistance they most need. (2) So that counselors and directors might understand these differences neither as the contrast between nature and grace, nor as a conflict between psychology and religion, nor as that of a positive spiritual experience and a negative psychological one. Rather, seeing differences within a framework of similarities reveals: (a) how grace works with and in human nature, (b) how an appropriate developmental model of the self enables counselors and directors to understand better the dynamics of depression and darkness, (c) how "positive disintegration" functions for the sake of greater psychological and religious maturity and transformation.

A. Note Differences: Prevent Mistaking Depression for Darkness

Could counselors and directors easily mistake depression for spiritual darkness? A counselor or director might confuse the two experiences if the depressed person presented her or his problem in religious language. For explicit concern about one's relationship to God is the outstanding feature of spiritual darkness. A religious person might deny the need for psychological help by explaining symptoms in "holy language" which seems to legitimate the situation. One might insist, for example, that "God is sending me this trial." Counselors or directors would, nevertheless, identify the problem as depression primarily by noting (1) seriously diminished ability to work or relate to others; (2) lack of energy available to persevere in attention to God in faith, hope, and charity; (3) need to "get out of" or "get over" this situation; (4) absence of deep peace. Ordinarily, depression is not presented as primarily a religious issue. Rather, it is experienced as a threat or questioning of oneself and the world.

B. Recognize Similarities While Noting Differences: Appreciate the Correlation Between Spirituality and Personal Maturity

There are many general similarities between depression and spiritual darkness because both are manifestations of a deep transition or "ground shift" in development toward maturity. Here maturity means growth toward both deeper relationships and greater self-direction (i.e. interiority), and it requires one to let go of the old way of making the meaning of oneself and others and construct a new way of doing this. These movements of letting go and constructing so that one may be both independent and related are common to both experiences. These common movements are, nevertheless, experienced and manifest in different ways in these two experiences. The explanation of these common movements will be organized in terms of similarities in the cause, characteristics, benefits, response to, and goal of depression and spiritual darkness. Within each explanation of similarities will be clarification of the differences between their manifestations in depression and those in spiritual darkness.

1. Causes

a. Cause Could Be One's Own Fault. While both depression and spiritual darkness could be caused through one's own fault, the fault would be different in each case. Whereas depression could result from one's choice to overwork or neglect one's health, a spiritual darkness which would more accurately be called "spiritual laxity" results from sinful choices or neglect of one's spiritual health through neglect of faith, hope, and charity. Both of these self-inflicted wounds should be distinguished from the painful, yet life-giving experiences which are the focus of this chapter.

b. Cause Could Be Beyond One's Control. The cause of both depression and spiritual darkness could, on the other hand, be primarily beyond one's control. Loss of a naturally therapeutic environment that was present at one time (e.g. parents, friends), or lack of a naturally therapeutic environment in society (e.g. sexism, racism) could bring on depression. It is always God's action in one's life that brings on spiritual darkness; yet this ultimate cause, John of the Cross maintains, comes to us *through* our ordinary life. God works through what we know and love. Therefore, God's transformation of our desires could be effected through events such as normal crises of life-span development, or renewal movements such as feminism. These expand one's horizon by raising new questions which one cannot yet answer, questions which one could not even imagine before these movements or events touched one's life. It is precisely through these events which shake one's understanding and challenge one's love that God can work to expand and, thus, tranform one's desires.

c. Cause Could Be Development Toward Maturity. When the cause of depression or spiritual darkness is the struggle of development toward maturity, there are signs which indicate that both experiences are manifestations of growth and life rather than death. Whereas the primary sign of growth in depression is desire to move out of the current phase, the principal sign of life in spiritual darkness is willingness to stay in this situation in order to cooperate with God's transforming action. In other words, both experiences can show signs of life but the signs are different.

If the following clues are present, a pastoral counselor or spiritual director could discern the type of depression which is a normal component of acute struggle for personal maturity. First, the depression is not completely debilitating. One retains some ability to relate and work, yet the person's focus is on difficulty. Second, the depression appears at a time of transition in life-span development; for example, one is leaving or entering a challenging relationship or task. Third, one manifests desire or ability to move out of the less mature phase; for example, one admits one's misery and wishes it would end.

If at least the following three signs are present together, one would discern not depression or spiritual laxity but growth emerging in spiritual darkness. There is a serious breakdown of communication with God and lack of satisfaction from spiritual things and from life in general. Nevertheless, there also is deep peace and a desire somehow to be attentive to God. In other words, one is willing to remain in this uncomfortable situation in order to cooperate with the hidden presence and transforming action of God's Spirit.

Using Kegan's psychological language, the developmental movement is out of "embeddedness" in relationships into greater self-direction, and then out of "embeddedness" in control into authentic intimacy and mutuality. In other words, greater maturity is greater capacity for differentiation *for the sake of* relationship. Using John of the Cross' language, one moves toward greater "perfection," understood as freer and more comprehensive love of God and all others in God. Both perspectives affirm the need for painful mental and emotional experience which is a kind of positive disintegration required for the sake of developing the capacity for greater love.

2. Characteristic Feelings, Behavior, Understanding

a. *Sadness and Fatigue.* Both depression and spiritual darkness are characterized by some degree of sadness and fatigue. But whereas one in depression regrets his inability to cope with his world as it has become, or regrets her loneliness, one in spiritual darkness may regret these same general things yet experience them precisely as aspects of one's relationship to God. While fatigue in depression is manifest in diminished ability to work or relate, the fatigue of spiritual darkness is infused with gentle energy for perseverance in loving attention to God and strength to keep working on one's spiritual life.

b. *Loss.* Both depression and spiritual darkness are experienced as loss of the "old," familiar way of making the meaning of self and others. We can see the correlation of human and spiritual development as we now examine the way psychological loss, in Kegan's model, is mirrored in the spiritual loss that is implied in John of the Cross' description of darkness. In adults, psychological loss is experienced in terms of the current developmental balance. Evolution out of the interpersonal balance entails loss of "self" as fused with others (insufficient differentiation in relationship), and loss of "other" as "part of me," as "who I am," not "whom I have relationship with." If the current balance is that of embeddedness in independence as control, movement toward maturity requires loss of "self" as controller of relationships and work (exaggerated differentiation in relationship), and loss of "other" as "whom/what I can control." Out of both types of loss comes the gain of greater capacity for mutuality and, therefore, for intimacy. In the former, the lack of psychic distance between self and other results in fusion which might be mistaken for intimacy. In the latter, exaggerated distance between self and other is a barrier to the mutuality necessary for intimacy. Suffering these losses, therefore, is actually the painful passage into human intimacy.

Spiritual loss is also experienced, according to John of the Cross, in terms of one's current phase of spiritual development. Expanding on John's insight, I notice parallels between Kegan's two types of adult loss and the transformation that John describes as spiritual darkness. Starting with the "other" that is lost, in darkness the "Other" that is lost is the God (God-image) with whom one is fused through conventional religion (i.e. socialization, unquestioning acceptance of religious formulations, psychological projection). For example, Annmarie lost God as "male." At this phase, one loses the "self" who securely feels and knows who God is and how God acts. At a more advanced phase of spiritual development, the "self" that must be lost is the "self" who has found some deeper meaning of God yet clings to this meaning, not yet able to grasp the "more" of God unless God "breaks one out" of this limited meaning and its accompanying limitation of love. Here the "Other" that is lost is the God one has "wrestled" with yet one somehow still underestimates and wants to control. As in Kegan's model of development, the benefit made possible by these losses is intimacy. John of the Cross is bold in his declaration that the aim and outcome of spiritual darkness is our "divinization." All darkness is really the inflowing of God's incomprehensible light, that is, the life which enables us to be weaned from fusion with God whom we love for the sake of self satisfaction or security, and be tranformed into a free adult who can love wtih God's own love! Such intimacy is beyond anything we could ask or imagine (Eph 3:20).

The loss of meaning of oneself and the world which John of the Cross associates with the severe "night of the spirit," is also, I notice, central to the more common "night of the senses." Both experiences are "dark" precisely because of the pain of loss of meaning. I believe that one reason why John identifies the special contemplative "night of the spirit" with loss of religious meaning is that his culture was so steeped in religion that severe doubt was unusual and associated with the extreme of atheism. In contemporary cultures with historical consciousness, on the other hand, doubting conventional religious meaning is more common and associated with movement toward more adult faith. Letting go of conventional religious assumptions may be more common now but it is not a less painful or difficult experience of spiritual darkness than the variety John describes as the "night of the senses."

c. Anger. Anger is a common element in depression and may be a good sign in the early phase of spiritual darkness. Depression often involves anger which is best understood as anger at the "old" self; indeed, it is an energetic way of defending against going back to the old balance. For example, anger expressed as anger at parents or friends who refuse to cooperate with immature behavior (e.g. parents who will not allow their married children to resolve arguments by coming home to mother and dad)—this anger is a defense against regression to fusion with parents. This indicates the beginning of evolution out of overidentification with parents. Complete fusion would be manifest not by anger but by feeling "hurt" and "dejected." The latter indicates that the person does not yet have the psychic separation which allows another, contrary viewpoint.

A person in spiritual darkness might also demonstrate maturity by expressing anger. For example, admitting anger at God for "doing this to me" is a good sign that one is defending against fusion with God who is an indulgent parent or a controlling parent. It allows for growth toward a more adult relationship of mutuality with God as Parent who promotes mature responsibility for one's life, or as Lover and Friend who relates with mutuality. An immature response would be exaggerated guilt (not honest admission of mistakes) or presumption that darkness is a punishment.

d. Threatened, Questioning. In both depression and spiritual darkness one feels threatened by one's inability to handle the new way one's world has become, or one radically questions both one's self and others. In depression, the assault on either the interpersonal balance (fusion) or the institutional balance (control) is experienced as threat or question arising from the simultaneous pull of vulnerability (to regression to the "old" balance) and doubt (about the validity of the emerging balance). For example, a woman might feel vulnerable because "others will devour me and use me," *and* doubt because "I'm selfish to be caring for my own needs." Here one is called to more mature relationships. Spiritual darkness is also rooted in questioning, but it is the questioning of one's religious self and world. There can be an early darkness, analogous to the interpersonal balance mentioned above, which is an assault on fusion with God who satisfies me. Here one feels threatened or one questions everything because the darkness is experienced as "losing one's faith" or "being abandoned by God," when one is really losing one's immature faith and being weaned from immature dependency on spiritual satisfaction so that one can evolve into more adult faith. One is now called to a choice for God beyond what is motivated by personal satisfaction or conventional religious approval. The deeper darkness, experienced as an assault on this adult faith, is felt as questioning all that gave prior meaning. Here one is called to "let go" with the adult surrender which became possible through the process of the earlier darkness.

3. Benefits of Depression and Darkness Which Promote Greater Maturity

a. Self-Knowledge. Clearly, both depression and spiritual darkness promote deeper understanding of one's self. In the first case, one gains knowledge of oneself as more than fusion with others and as more than control of work and relationships. In spiritual darkness one gains knowledge of oneself as affirmed by God as an adult who must trust one's own religious experience and who is free to love in new, unfamiliar ways. In the darkness which is analogous to the deeper human maturity described by Kegan, one knows that surrender of a mature self is far from the childlike obedience which is conformity to another's will. This surrender is the free relinquishing of complete self-direction in order to enjoy mutuality and authentic intimacy.

b. Freedom. Freedom is a significant outcome of both depression and spiritual darkness. Struggle with depression issues in freedom from immature fusion, or freedom from the restricting control which blocks human intimacy. Fidelity in spiritual darkness issues in freedom from adherence to the "idolatrous" God of one's images or projections. Or, as spiritual development continues, darkness allows freedom from the limits of all one's fears and ego boundaries which prevent one from loving with God's own love.

4. Support for Growth Requires an Environment of Confirmation, Contradiction, and Continuity

a. Confirmation. One suffering depression or spiritual darkness is helped by a pastoral counselor or spiritual director (and a wider social context) who confirms those human capacities for relationship and independence which are present yet still immature. In both cases, the helper confirms love but not fusion, free commitment but not control. In spiritual direction, moreover, the focus is on discerning the action of God's Spirit so that one may respond in ways which confirm, that is, cooperate with the direction of that action.

b. Contradiction. A pastoral counselor or spiritual director helps one in depression or spiritual darkness by contradicting immature ways of making the meaning of "self" and "other" according to that person's developmental phase. In both cases, the helper would contradict refusal to claim one's own desires, or would refuse to accept non-intimate relationships which retreat from vulnerability and mutuality. In spiritual direction, moreover, the emphasis is on contradicting whatever God seems to be calling one to leave behind. For example, John of the Cross advises spiritual directors to contradict a person's determination to stay with familiar methods of prayer when these methods now result in frustration. For John of the Cross as well as for Robert Kegan, this contradiction is actually a way of freeing the person to risk entering a new, more complex way of loving and knowing.

c. Continuity. Support for persons in depression and spiritual darkness comes from continuing to be their companion so that they may reintegrate the helping person into their newer, more mature relationships. In spiritual direction, however, the primary continuity comes from God whose fidelity never falters. Nevertheless, the human fidelity of counselors and spiritual directors is essential and serves also as a healing revelation of God's love for the person in depression or darkness.

C. Conclusion: The Goal of Both Experiences Is Intimacy and Equality

The primary goal of both spiritual darkness and depression's implicit developmental tension is intimacy. Depression is a manifestation of positive disintegration which occurs for the sake of deeper relationship. For example, breakdown of fusion allows differentiation of the self which permits a more complex relationship. Or relaxation of control permits mutuality and, therefore, authentic intimacy. Spiritual darkness, too, is always a process of movement into deeper, more authentic intimacy with God and with all other persons in God. This intimacy is analogous to the human maturity described by Kegan, an experience of equality. The amazing truth is that John of the Cross affirms that the closer one comes to God, the more equality there is between God and the human person. Experiencing the reality of the fourth gospel in which Jesus declares that "As the Father has loved me, I also love you," John of the Cross teaches that spiritual darkness occurs so that one becomes divinized and capable of loving with God's own love. In other words, God desires and effects our "equality" with God.

Notes

[1]Texts cited as CWJC are from Kavanaugh and Rodriguez (1973) which has a North American English prose style. Peers (1953) has a British style.

[2]An accurate, popular description of depression addressed to women from an evangelical perspective is Poinsette (1984). Fairchild (1980) is a pastoral guide on this topic.

References

Bootzin, Richard and Acocella, Joan Ross. *Abnormal Psychology.* New York: Random House, 4th ed., 1984.

Buckley, Michael. "The Structure of the Rules for Discernment of Spirits." *The Way* 20 (1973): 19–37.

The Collected Works of St. John of the Cross. Translated by Kieran Kavanaugh and Otilio Rodriguez. Washington, D.C.: Institute for Carmelite Studies, 1973. 2nd ed., 1979.

The Complete Works of Saint John of the Cross. Translated and edited by E. Allison Peers. New ed., ref. 3 vols. Westminster, MD: Newman Press, 1953. Reprinted by Sheed & Ward, 1 vol., 1978.

Fairchild, Roy W. *Finding Hope Again: A Pastor's Guide to Counseling Depressed Persons.* San Francisco: Harper & Row, 1980.

FitzGerald, Constance. Lectures on John of the Cross given to the graduate course, "Classics of Western Christian Spirituality," at The Catholic University of America, March 1985. unpublished.

FitzGerald, Constance. "Impasse and Dark Night." In Joann Wolski Conn, ed. *Women's Spirituality.* New York: Paulist, 1986. pp. 287–311.

FitzGerald, Constance. "A Discipleship of Equals—Voices from Tradition: Teresa of Avila and John of the Cross." In Francis A. Eigo, ed. *A Discipleship of Equals: Toward a Christian Feminist Spirituality.* vol. 20 (1987). *Proceedings of the Villanova Theology Institute.* Villanova, PA: Villanova University, 1988.

John of the Cross: Selected Writings. Edited with an introduction by Kieran Kavanaugh. The Classics of Western Spirituality. New York: Paulist, 1987.

Kegan, Robert. *The Evolving Self.* Cambridge, MA: Harvard, 1982.

Miller, Jean Baker. *Toward a New Psychology of Women.* Boston: Beacon, 1976.

Miller, Jean Baker. "The Development of Women's Sense of

Self.'' *Work in Progress Papers #12.* Wellesley, MA: The Stone Center, 1987.

Poinsette, Brenda. *Understanding a Woman's Depression.* Wheaton, IL: Tyndale House, 1984.

Schneiders, Sandra M. *Women and the Word.* New York: Paulist, 1986.

Thérèse of Lisieux. *Story of a Soul.* Translated by John Clarke. Washington, D.C.: Institute of Carmelite Studies, 1975.

Conclusion

Years of receiving and giving the ministry of spiritual direction as well as teaching students in Neumann College's graduate pastoral counseling program have convinced me that Christian spirituality and personal maturity are identical in basic ways. This conviction can be grasped consistently on both theoretical and practical levels, however, only if spiritual and psychological development are seen to have the same goal or model of maturity. Therefore, presenting and evaluating a model of development which promotes such integration has been the aim of this book.

The first step in this project was a survey of Christian spirituality focused on the way tradition understands maturity. While there is great diversity, a consistent theme is maturity perceived as loving relationship to God and others. In Catholic tradition, relationship to God never canceled human freedom or responsible decision despite strong emphasis on obedience and surrender. Within theologies of discernment and spiritual darkness, especially, tradition honored reliance on one's own religious experience and cautioned against mere conformity to conventional wisdom. In these themes, therefore, contemporary Christians can find support for modern concern with adult self-direction or autonomy. To use contemporary language, autonomy for the sake of a more complex and mutual relationship with God and others can be noted as a constant theme in the tradition of Christian spirituality.

Next, the book moved to find a model of psychological maturity which could be integrated with spirituality's insistence on relationship as the goal of maturity. A genuine search was needed because most psychology places primary value on autonomy and, in practice, speaks of attachment and relationship in the language of repression or as warning signs of imma-

168

turity. It is the recent work of Carol Gilligan and other feminist psychologists that radically questioned prevailing assumptions. Thus, Chapter 2 clarified and evaluated Gilligan's model of maturity as relationship. Given the inability of Gilligan's theory to provide a comprehensive model useful for counseling and spiritual direction with women and men, the search continued.

A more comprehensive model was found (Chapter 3) in Robert Kegan's constructive view of the evolving self. Kegan incorporated feminist views by valuing both relationship and autonomy as intrinsic to maturity at every stage of development. Demonstrating this model's value for pastoral counseling was the next task (Chapter 4) followed by the chapter which widened the evaluation of Kegan's model to include its significance for spiritual direction (Chapter 5). At this point (Chapter 6) the integration of spirituality, psychology and theology was evident on both theoretical and practical levels. For here all the issues of the book were concentrated on the struggle and pain of moving from one phase of maturity to another. Spirituality and human maturity were shown to be inextricably bound together in both spiritual darkness and psychological depression. Both experiences were seen to be necessary and inevitable breakthroughs into authentic maturity: intimacy grounded in self-direction or differentiation for the sake of mutual relationship with God and others.

Implications. First, this book's conclusions imply that Christians need not be afraid or suspicious of human nature, emotions, or the ambiguity and struggles of human development. God works through every aspect of our life, even in those we may have been taught to see as obstacles to God: our sins and failures. This does not mean that everything automatically deepens our relationship to God; but everything could and can deepen it if we have a model of maturity which helps us recognize and use life for growth in intimacy with God and everything in the universe as connected with God. Second, the book demonstrates that growth in faith comes through the *ordinary* aspects of life. Nothing extraordinary is needed as a "sign" or "proof" of God's creative presence to us. God's Spirit works "wonders" in all our lives, but they are accomplished precisely through the normal patterns, crises, breakdowns and break-throughs of our work, study, family, and care for friends and strangers. One never needs to search after unusual experiences or places in order to experience the revelation of God. Emphasis on the ordinary harmonizes with the gospel warning that God's revelation in Jesus was overlooked by those who considered Jesus as too ordinary (Mk 6). On the same theme, Mark's gospel shows that Jesus' "powerful deeds" produced fear or anxiety but never produced faith. In Mark's gospel, faith was manifest only by one who could see God's action in Jesus' obscurity and failure (Mk 15). Third, in practical terms, for counselors and spiritual directors, the integration explained in this book means that concentration on each ministry's special focus—human growth or spiritual development—inevitably promotes and involves a person's comprehensive development. Immersion in the human is immersion in God's presence and action in us.

Challenges for Future Work. I hope the practice of spiritual direction will receive the level of sustained reflection and evaluation that now characterizes the field of pastoral counseling. I am not advocating use of pastoral counseling as the primary model for training or supervision in direction. Rather, as I have demonstrated in Chapter 6, I believe that theological sources offer the most appropriate models for the spiritual direction process. For example, although the tradition of Ignatius Loyola is taught more widely and systematically than any other theoretical framework, this book uses the Carmelite tradition in a systematic way. We need further study of how, *in practice,* these traditions can be integrated for spiritual direction.

I also encourage pastoral ministers to persevere in the arduous task of recovering the tradition in a way that supports feminist issues. For example, this book contributes to the recovery of traditions which promote mutuality and equality between women and men, clergy and laity. For another example, this book is written, obviously, from my own perspective as a Christian feminist who has ministered primarily, though not exclusively, with women. We need men's description of how feminist issues affect their process in spiritual direction.

A most urgent challenge is the need to explore social structures as a regular component of discernment. Cases in this book use feminist theology and psychology as critical tools for noticing, evaluating, and replacing sexist attitudes which are institutionalized, for example, in marriage, education, and training for pastoral ministry. Institutional structures are described here in psychological terms such as "culture of embeddedness" and "naturally therapeutic environment." But whether the terms are psychological, sociological, or theological, social analysis must now accompany discernment's traditional emphasis on the individual. For the most effective, integrated pastoral ministry cooperates with both the personal and the social transformation now being directed by God's Spirit.